MANAGEMENT DECISION MAKING

MANAGEMENT DECISION MAKING

John Adair

Gower

© John Adair 1985

Published by
Gower Publishing Company Limited,
Gower House,
Croft Road,
Aldershot,
Hants GU11 3HR,
England.

British Library Cataloguing in Publication Data

Adair, John
  Management decision making.
  1. Decision-making
  I. Title
  658.4'03   HD30.23

ISBN 0–566–02530–2

Typeset in Great Britain by
Guildford Graphics Limited, Guildford, Surrey.
Printed and bound in Great Britain
by Billings & Sons Limited, Worcester.

Contents

		page
Acknowledgements		viii
Preface		ix
1	**The management context**	1

The crucial competence — The rational manager —
The five point plan — Some factors which affect
decision making — How managers spend their time
— Chief resource or bloody nuisance? — People are
wholes, not spare parts — Involving work people in
decisions

| 2 | **Know your mind** | 20 |

Brain power — Three families of abilities — Using
your depth mind — Managing emotion – Roadblocks
to learning — Conclusion

| 3 | **Analysing** | 29 |

Identifying the hallmarks of a good analytical mind

— Analytical ability in management — The skill of asking yourself questions — The analytical methods of logicians — Think backwards — Organise the facts — The logic of the situation — The Missing Missile

4 **Holistic thinking**   49
The holistic vision — Some holistic approaches — Thinking holistically about problems — Nature and growth — Holistic numeracy — Signpost

5 **Thinking in concepts**   58
Concepts — Conceptual thinking and decision making — Reflective thinking — Conclusions

6 **Imaginative thinking**   69
Thinking in pictures — Thinking and imagination — Imaginative thinking in action — Yes, but can you develop imaginative thinking? — Imagination in perspective

7 **Valuing**   82
The autonomy of valuing — A policy for thinkers — Consulting specialists — Valuing in perspective

8 **Your sixth sense – intuition**   92
Trusting your intuition — Emotion and intuition — Business flair — Conclusion

9 **Your depth mind**   100
Using the principle — Some guidelines

10 **Options**   107
Developing a range of options — False assumptions: some examples from history — Some limitations affecting management choices — Generating more options — Assessing the consequences — The importance of probability — Summary

11 **Arguing**   123
How to get it wrong — Conclusion

12 **Useful originality**   138
What is creativity? — Necessity is the mother of

invention — Widen your span of analogy — The
depth mind dimension — Idea banks — Innovation
— Management actions

13 Developing your thinking skills 153
What is an effective decision? — The goal of
consensus — What is an effective thinker? — Making
an inventory of your skills — Learning on the job —
Keep mentally fit — How to avoid stimulus deficiency
— Conclusion

Answers to problems 166

Index 175

Acknowledgements

The following publishers were kind enough to give permission for the reproduction of copyright material:

Punch Publications Ltd: the cartoons in Chapters 1, 3, 6, 8, 10 and 12.

William Collins Sons & Co. Ltd: the extract from *Back from the Brink* by Sir Michael Edwardes (used in Chapter 5).

Weidenfeld and Nicolson Ltd: the extract from *Return to Go* by Jim Slater (used in Chapter 13).

Hamish Hamilton Ltd: the extracts from *After I was Sixty* by Lord Thomson (1975) used in Chapters 4, 9, 11 and 12.

Preface

Decision making is an essential function of management. Together with leadership and communication it heads the list of those abilities which as a manager you should be seeking to develop. The purpose of this book is to help you do just that.

The actual moment of decision cannot be studied. Sometimes you are not even conscious of it. Our primary concern therefore must be the whole process by which minds are made up, the mental movements which lead to decisions: in a word, thinking.

The kind of thinking which leads to action should be regarded by the manager as a demanding activity in its own right. 'If I have any advice to pass on it is this: if one wants to be successful one must think until it hurts'. So wrote Roy Thomson, one of the great businessmen of our times. 'Believe me', he added, 'this is hard work and, from my close observation, I can say that there are few people indeed who are prepared to perform this arduous and tiring work'.

Deciding implies choice from several – or many – possibilities.

Thinking is the preliminary work of weighing up the pros and cons for each course of action. A decisive person is one who has the power to stop thinking and start acting.

Decision making of this nature should not exhaust the manager's thinking time. For one thing, it assumes that you know what is your objective: the mark you are trying to hit. That is not always the case. There is a perennial need in organisations to 'think until it hurts' about their purpose, aims and objectives.

Another important sphere for thinking which is not coupled to daily decisions concerns the generation of new ideas. Inventing new products, services and technologies, modifying or improving existing ones, seeing new opportunities and discovering fresh markets requires a capacity for original thinking. Here, too much preoccupation with decisions can actually be counter productive.

On this sketchmap we now need to place the sort of thinking appropriate to management which is commonly called problem solving. A problem means literally something thrown in front of you which requires attention, solution or answer. It is a very general word, as is shown by the very varied ways we use it in everyday life: Jack's drinking problem, the problem of unemployment, the problem of motivating people, the problem of inflation, and so on.

Problems in these cases are loose descriptions of states of affairs that call for decision. Thus decision making and problem solving as activities tend to be conflated with each other; indeed much management literature seems to regard them as synonymous. I feel that this is a mistake.

The manager, I suggest, may be faced with two broad types of problem. The first are like obstacles in his path. He has decided his objective and chosen his course of action: somewhere along the road he encounters an unforeseen block, such as a strike in a supplier's factory or the unexpected illness of a key colleague. What should he do? Problems of this sort derive from decisions. If you never decide anything you never have any problems. The mental processes for dealing with them are identical to decision making.

The second type of problem concerns systems. Something goes wrong with a mechanical system such as an assembly line or machinery. Then the problem-solver has to act like the doctor dealing with the human body; he has to study the symptoms and diagnose the underlying cause or causes of the trouble. Only when these have been corrected will the health of the system be restored. Problem solving of this kind is heavily dependent on professional knowledge and case experience. As a manager rises higher it is an activity he usually has to delegate to specialists. For these reasons problem solving in systems situations is not a major theme in this book, although I have discussed it elsewhere*.

We can solve many problems – crossword puzzles, for example – without having to take action. But decision implies action and change: life will not be quite the same again and it may very well be radically different. Thus people who are very clever at solving academic-type problems may lack the qualities required to take decisions in situations involving uncertainty and risk.

The context of decision making for the manager is the subject of the first chapter. In it I contrast the theory of the rational manager with some research into what managers actually do, mainly to get you thinking hard about how you use your time. Also in this chapter I underline the significance of decision making.

The subsequent chapters review the basic functions of thinking – analysing, reasoning, synthesising and thinking in wholes, conceptualising, imagining and valuing. These are described and illustrated with practical examples and case studies. For, where possible, I have drawn on the experience of those who have excelled in decision making or some other relevant form of thinking. Not all examples are taken from business: you can stretch your mind if you consider a wide range of analogies or models. To stimulate further thought I have included some exercises and activities for you to tackle as you go through the book.

In Chapter 9 I explore the role of what I call the 'depth mind' in decision making, an aspect of thinking which has received too little attention in the management textbooks. You can make progress in making more effective use of the unconscious mind if you are aware of its existence and understand how it works.

---

*Chapter 5, *Training for Decisions* (1971), reproduced in *The Skills of Leadership* (Gower, 1984).

Following that, in the later chapters of the book, I focus upon decision making in the sense of choosing between feasible options; the nature of good reasoned argument about those courses of action; and how new ideas are produced. The final chapter is a summary, drawing together the threads and suggesting practical ways in which to maintain and improve your basic mental fitness.

If managerial thinking is not an entirely solitary activity nor is writing about it. I am conscious of the debt I owe to past thinkers and writers in this field, too many to mention here but their names will appear in the text. I am especially grateful to those who have contributed directly by reading and commenting constructively and critically upon the first draft. Bernard Babington Smith, until his retirement Senior Lecturer in Experimental Psychology and a Fellow of Pembroke College in Oxford University, has long been a source of ideas and inspiration for me in this area and, having read my manuscript, gave me a characteristically kind and reflective but searching tutorial on it, page by page. Ron Pittendrigh, Senior Training Manager in Thorn-EMI, also read the manuscript and added useful comments. Roger Oldcorn, Senior Lecturer in Business Development at Kingston Regional Management Centre and author of the first-class introduction to management in the Pan Breakthrough series, worked through the text and made a number of valuable suggestions which I have been delighted to incorporate. My respective editors at Gower and Pan – Malcolm Stern and Steven Mair – have helped shape the book for publication. Jennifer Perraton has typed the various drafts for me with her customary skill. Lastly, my wife Thea read it through to check the sense as well as the style. To all of these friends and helpers I give my warmest thanks.

John Adair

1 The management context

Thinking is not done in a vacuum. This book assumes a context: the manager at work.

Managers are subject to many pressures. They are interacting with their environment with particular ends in view. But that environment is subject to change; so are the ends of enterprise and so are the managers themselves. Therefore thinking for the manager is like handling a small ship in a rough sea, often without maps or charts. That is true management.

In this chapter we shall survey the key factors that impinge upon – and often shape – the decision making aspect of the manager's job. Perhaps you will recognise yourself in this identikit picture. In the rest of the book we shall work on that picture until it becomes more to your liking.

What is management? All authors like to start with a definition. It is easier to say what it is not. It is certainly not a science. Management does not stand on the same footing as, for example, physics or chemistry. The search for a comparable knowledge base, however, has been far from fruitless. We do know some things about managers.

The crucial competence

Everyone agrees that decision making and problem solving are among the core functions of the manager's job. By 'everyone' I mean the academics who have studied management and the practitioners who manage. Let us concentrate upon the latter.

In 1976 a questionnaire was sent to 200 leaders of industry and commerce. They included the executive heads (chairman, managing director or chief executive) of the largest – by size of turnover – 163 industrial companies in Britain. To these were added the heads of the nationalised industries and the leaders of the clearing banks, main merchant banks, building societies and other financial institutions. Just on 60 per cent replied, a high response for such a survey. In one of the questions, the executive heads were asked to rank 25 attributes most valuable at the top level of management. In first place they put *the ability to take decisions*.

One of the most sensible criteria we have for determining pay relativities is to go by the decision making content of jobs. A surgeon, an airline pilot and a refuse collector all take decisions. Why do we pay the first two more than the latter? Because their decisions involve life-and-death for us and because the knowledge required for their jobs takes many years to acquire. When a client complained to a famous painter about the fee he proposed to charge her for six hours of work on her portrait he replied, 'Not six hours, madam, but thirty years of experience'.

A builder responsible for a large town centre redevelopment, lasting three years, will earn more salary than one who merely modifies kitchens. You are going to be paid in life by the quality and quantity of the decisions you make within your sphere of work.

Therefore decisions are central to managing. One definition of management is 'deciding what to do and getting it done'. In any management situation a decision or series of decisions must precede implementation. The outcome in terms of success or failure, however, will depend on both the decision itself and your

2

effectiveness in implementing it. That is where leadership or influencing, communication and motivation come into play. The first requirement for success in any enterprise, then, is high quality management decisions.

The rational manager

The decision maker, in the classic view of management, follows a logical or step-by-step sequence. He is completely rational. He has clear, unconflicting objectives and a perfect knowledge of the problem. All information is gathered and all possible solutions or courses considered.

In management theory the hallmark of the rational manager is that he makes a decision between choices in terms of their *consequences* or outcomes. When people talk about being rational in this context that is usually what they mean. If the objective is purely financial – to maximise your profit – consequences can be assessed numerically and a simple choice made. If you can safely invest a large sum of money with a ten per cent return in one stock or with twelve per cent in another, the choice is obvious – at least on purely rational grounds.

The rational manager in action

Imagine you are the owner of a small building firm. One day, you are told that the old lorry you have been using for the last eight years is on the point of falling to bits. You have at most a month to decide what to do. Here is a list of possible actions you can take. Which would you not do, and in what order would you work on the remaining items:

1 Go and buy a new lorry from the nearest dealer.
2 Take a month's holiday in Spain.
3 Buy a farm instead.
4 Find out the cost of renting new vans of different types.
5 Work out what kind of lorry you need.
6 Ask the bank manager how much he will lend you.
7 Add up how much money you could afford to spend.

3

8 Find out the tax angles.
9 Get details of all possible types of suitable lorry, including price, fuel consumption etc.
10 Get three quotes for repairing your present lorry.
11 Take a cold bath.
12 Sell the business.
13 Carefully evaluate all your options.
14 Consult your staff.
15 Find out the cost of hay and a horse and cart.

The irrelevant items in the list are numbers 2, 3, 11 and 15. The information gained and the activity of tackling these items may be interesting and enjoyable but they are not vital to the decision. Whereas the remaining items are most certainly important.

The rational manager would start by defining the problem, in this case whether to buy a new lorry or repair the old one. Then he would obtain all the relevant information (items 4, 6, 7, 8, 9) and he would need to draw up a list of all the reasonable alternatives available to him (item 13). Having evaluated the options he would take his decision and take some kind of action. This may be to sell the business or buy a new lorry from the nearest dealer or even do nothing! The important point is that the decision is taken at the right time and is the best possible choice. What about consulting his staff? That depends on the style of the owner; some always consult, some never consult.

The five point plan

On numerous occasions in courses on decision making I have asked managers to list the main stages they go through when making a decision or solving a problem. There is a general agreement which clusters around a five point plan, as shown in Table 1.1.

There is probably an element of unreality in the five point plan in that the several thousands of managers who answered the question may have been telling me what *ought* to happen, rather than what actually *does* happen. They may have attended courses or read books on the subject, and both sources preach the five point plan.

Table 1.1

Steps	Key points
Define objective	Specifying the aim or objective, having recognised the need for a decision
Collect information	Collecting and organising data; checking facts and opinions; identifying possible causes; establishing time constraints and other criteria.
Develop options	Listing possible courses of action; generating ideas.
Evaluate and decide	Listing the pros and cons; examining the consequences; measuring against criteria; trials; testing against objective; selecting the best.
Implement	Acting to carry out the decision; monitoring the decision; reviewing.

Nonetheless it is significant that there is a consensus on this sequence. It means you can appeal to it in joint decision making or problem solving. It can serve as a frame of reference for a team working together. Moreover, it does reflect what many managers in many situations actually try to do.

Figure 1.1 shows a slightly expanded version of the five point plan. 'Sensing effects' means having the awareness which picks up the signs or symptoms of an existing problem, long before the nature of the problem is clear.

If you happen to have attended a decision making meeting in the last week try and recollect how far its chairman guided the group in the five phases. Alternatively, if you are involved in making a personal decision yourself, write it down as far as you can, using the five point plan as a framework.

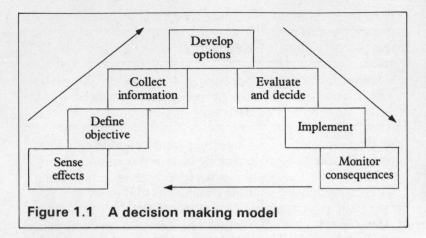

Figure 1.1   A decision making model

Some factors which affect decision making

Managers have to take into account a wider range of consequences of possible courses of action than the management science approach in its early days assumed. An American researcher called Nicholas Nicholaidis analysed 332 administrative decisions by officials in the public sector. Far from decisions being based purely on logical grounds, he found strong admixtures of emotion, power politics, the influence of other people and the individual decision makers' own values. Moreover, the decision makers rarely settled for the best or optimum solution as recommended by the management text-books, tending to look for a satisfactory compromise among two or more of the courses or solutions, i.e. one that:

- agreed, at least to some extent, with their own personal interests, values and needs
- met the value standards of their supervisors
- was acceptable to both those who would be affected by the decision and those who had to carry it out
- looked reasonable in its context
- contained a built-in justification which would furnish an excuse, and possibly an avenue of retreat, in case the actual results of the decision turned out to be quite different from those anticipated.

How far Nicholaidis was an accurate and fair observer is open to debate, but this research is typical of much which emphasises the apparently illogical elements at work in the manager's thinking, such as the presence of strong emotion and the influence of personal values.

There is one factor that especially militates against a careful step-by-step approach to decision making – there is often not enough time. So you cannot gather all the important and relevant information, nor carry out a thorough evaluation of the choices. Managers agree that there often seems to be insufficient 'thinking time'.

The prominence of such phrases as 'influence of other people', and 'power politics' points to another missing key factor in the classic view of managerial decision making – the centrality of people. That is the theme of the next chapter. But it is worth noting now that taking the human factor into consideration does not necessarily imply that you are flying in the face of reason.

Rational thinking can also be contrasted with the kind of decision which seems to be taken without conscious reasoning or in spite of the five step plan rather than through it.

The Case of the Rolling Cameras

A television crew filmed the course of a decision by the British Steel Corporation. Condensing many months of discussion into several hours of film, it followed the decision making process through committees, conferences and meetings in corridors. The resulting film was shown without commentary on the national network.

The choices before the Corporation were ones which any Monopoly-playing viewer could understand. They were negotiating with a German firm, Willi Korf, about an iron-ore processing plant. They could buy two for £43 million, one for £26 million, or do without.

Although the project had been under discussion for months, the day before the contract deadline not all the top executives were convinced that the new processing plant was needed.

The climax came at a monthly board meeting when a scheme for two plants was finally agreed. The then Chairman, Sir Monty Finniston, had, it seemed, leaned in this direction all along. Lionel

Pugh, the finance director and the one articulate dissenter, tore up his brief with eloquent finality.

The austerely professional film left out the context of the decision. The unions and the Government, for example, were barely mentioned in the programme, yet their view on building a large installation on the Clyde must have been known. But as an illustration of organisation men at work it was accurate and fascinating. It captured the tendency of managers to talk in their own jargon, often an enemy to clear thinking.

The impression given about how Britain's largest nationalised industry planned its business was hardly encouraging. According to a report in a national newspaper a few days later, Luke McLoughlin, chairman of the workers action committee at Shotton steel works in North Wales, called for the dismissal of Sir Monty Finniston. The steel industry, he said, had been thoroughly disgusted by the filmed meeting of the Steel Corporation Board. 'The community now knows that major decisions within the Corporation are taken to meet the whims and fancies of the chairman'.

How managers spend their time

New light is shed on managerial decision making by research into how managers spend their time. These researchers use methods similar to those used successfully to study animals in the field, especially endangered species.

"Look, we've been on this for a month now—are we or aren't we going to admit TV cameras to our decision-making process?"

Early research by Dr Rosemary Stewart asked 160 British managers to keep an exact diary of their activities over a four week period.[1] The average manager worked 42½ hours per week, spending three-quarters of it in his own establishment. About half of the total working week was spent in his own office. As Table 1.2 shows, a great deal of time was spent with other people.

Table 1.2

Average proportion of managers' time spent on various activities

	Percentage
Informal discussions	43
Paperwork	36
Committees	7
Telephone	6
Inspection of others	6
Social activities	4

Stewart reported that managers often complain that 'it's one damn thing after another' and that 'there is no time to think'. During the month the average manager had only nine periods of half an hour long when he was not interrupted. A typical day is one in which he is attempting to cover thirteen widely different tasks – problems or decisions – while having as many fleeting contacts in person or on the telephone with subordinates, colleagues and, occasionally, superiors.

Of course the 'average manager' embraces wide variations among the actual managers studied. Some managers spend much of their time away from their companies, visiting customers or attending conferences and exhibitions. Sales managers are frequently in this group. Others sit longer at their desks dealing with paperwork. Trouble-shooters, such as works managers and production managers, experience an exceptionally fragmented day with much time spent in coping with crises and finding speedy solutions. Personnel managers spend a much longer time than average in committees and are constantly discussing matters with other people, especially colleagues.

You will notice that *all* managers spend a lot of time talking to other people, usually in short, informal conversations. Tom Burns, in 1957, found that executives spent up to 80 per cent of their time in this way. Virtually all studies show that unscheduled discussions and interruptions are characteristic of such work.

Summarising much of the previous evidence in 1971 together with the results of his own survey of the work of five executive heads, Henry Mintzberg argued that the main conclusion to be drawn is that executive work is characterised by variety, fragmentation and brevity. Businessmen perform a great variety of tasks at a high pace and with little time to spare.[2] Half the tasks in Mintzberg's sample lasted less than nine minutes: only 10 per cent lasted more than one hour. 'Superficiality is an occupational hazard of the manager's job'. Networks of contacts were important: oral and face-to-face encouters – programmed or unprogrammed – were preferred to paperwork. It was the nature of the job that top executives were constantly disturbed from scheduled tasks – and they appeared to like it. They were not 'reflective planners, but adaptable information manipulators who prefer the live, concrete situation'.

If this insight of Mintzberg is correct, books or courses designed to turn managers into the rational stereotype are bound to fail. Managers are action-centred, short-term and concrete in their thinking. They have, like prisoners, grown accustomed to their chains; they refuse to leave the treadmill of activity – it has become an end in itself.

This fragmented day is not the inevitable consequence of the manager's job. It is not the way executives *have* to work. It is partly the consequence of personal and corporate ineffectiveness – and it may lead to ineffectiveness too. How many *successful* top managers in private industry or public service can you think of who are operating in this way – all action and no thought?

Mintzberg's own proposed solution was to suggest a downgrading of the importance of formal decision making as presented by the management science approach. He put forward a reclassification, based on three groups of role:

- *interpersonal* – action as figurehead, providing leadership and liaison;
- *informational* – monitoring, dissemination, spokesman;
- *decisional* – entrepreneur, disturbance handler, resource allocation, negotiation.

Work in the first group is more important than the classical model of the manager as primarily a rational decision maker allows. As Stewart showed, some top and middle-level executives spend over 40 per cent of their time with people outside their units. As for the second cluster of roles, Mintzberg's own research showed that 40 per cent of the time which chief executives spent in contact with others went solely upon communicating information. (Of course that information may relate to decisions – past, present or future.)

This high pressure *ad hoc* coping and fire-fighting behaviour can be stressful.

The Executive Monkey

In one unpleasant experiment carried out in 1958 at the Walter Reed Army Institute of Research in America, two monkeys were kept in 'restraining chairs' (in which they could move their heads and limbs but not their bodies), both with a bar in front of them. One of the monkeys, called the Executive Monkey, had to learn to press his bar at least every five seconds, otherwise both he and his partner in the next cage received an electric shock. The other monkey's bar had no effect at all on producing a shock. Thus both monkeys were on the receiving end of identical shock experiences, but only the Executive Monkey had control. He was the one who had to remain alert and to act appropriately in order to avoid the shocks.

When the monkeys were placed in this experimental situation for six hour work periods and six hour rest periods between each experimental session, daily physiological tests did not detect any abnormalities in either monkey. Both monkeys maintained a proper diet and weight. After 23 days, however, the Executive Monkey died. The cause of death was ulcers. The experiment was repeated with another pair of monkeys.

Although both sets of monkeys in these experiments received

identical shock experiences, the second monkey in each case remained perfectly healthy. The Executive Monkey differed from his partner in that he had to make constant decisions. Having control seems to be the critical factor in stress. It is not simply being faced with a painful event; stress is only produced when the organism must develop some way of coping with a threatening situation.

What looms large as a threat will vary from person to person. Making a parachute jump can be less alarming than having to make a speech. Threat and uncertainty experienced in combination over prolonged periods of time tend to produce some well-defined physiological symptoms in most of us.

Stress and work pressure are not the same. Most top quality managers, like other top performers, love working under pressure. Adrenalin is addictive. Even threat and danger in mild doses can be stimulating. But the work pattern of the over-busy, over-active manager is one factor which may combine with others to produce real stress.

Take the element of uncertainty. In a national sample taken of United States male workers, it was found that feeling unsure of their expected role at work was a source of stress for many. Uncertainty over their scope and responsibilities troubled 35 per cent; 29 per cent were bothered by the ambiguity of their co-workers' expectations; and 32 per cent disliked being unsure of their superior's evaluations.

If work pressure becomes stress, through the admixture of such factors as personal threat and prolonged uncertainty, and perhaps through the accidental addition of other unwanted changes either personal – falling sick, matrimonial troubles, the death of a loved one – or at work – labour troubles, failing products, law suits, international currency problems, tax difficulties – you must expect the quality of an executive's rational thinking and his powers of decision taking to fall dramatically. This works in reverse too: sometimes an executive's inability to take a decision has been known to lead to serious illness, through worry.

Professor Norman Dixon catalogued this cause-and-effect syndrome in the military field but it applies also to managers. 'Under stress some people become indecisive and vacillating.

Rather than make a decision they put off the evil moment until overtaken by events. Others, unable to tolerate suspense, act impulsively without waiting to weigh the odds or consider the options'.[3] Giving the power of choice to committees, incidentally, is not the answer. It has been claimed, for example, that the four worst decisions in the whole of American military history were the products of 'group think'.

People with the very qualities which enable them to reach positions involving important decisions – such as burning ambition, the desire to achieve and the capacity to work intensely hard – are the very ones who are most vulnerable to 'stimulus overload'. They may also fall victim to the kind of stress that can create such physical disorders as hypertension and coronary disease, and, more seriously, impair their thinking abilities and the quality of their decisions.

* * * * *

To summarise so far, the essence of management is decision making. In the classic view that process involves the five step plan: define objective, collect information, develop alternatives, evaluate and decide, and implement. A rational approach to management emphasises the importance of making the best choice by calculating the consequences. That is fine so long as you remember that the consequences which managers should consider are not solely financial: other benefits and losses must enter the picture. Moreover, many managers do not appear to reach decisions by a logical or step-by-step process. They rely more on flair and intuition. Indeed there are pressures on the manager, such as shortage of time, which work against him following a systematic decision making process. These pressures can conspire to induce stress, which in turn can lead to poor quality thinking and indecisiveness. Time to think must be the priority for the manager who wants to become more effective, and therefore he must manage his time with that end in view.

Chief resource or bloody nuisance?

'It is not the business that is difficult, it is the people', an experienced manager said to me. A younger manager put it more

13

forcefully: 'People are just a bloody nuisance in this factory. The sooner we go over to robotics the better'. These attitudes are in sharp contrast to those of other managers and in classical management doctrine. But they do reflect something of reality. People can be difficult to manage. But they are also the enterprise's most valuable resource. Business, even a one-man business, is co-operative effort. Management implies that you have people working under you, and probably beside you and above you. In the classic definition, management is achieving results through people.

Because other people are so central to the manager, in contrast to, say, a fur trapper, author, cartoonist, research scientist or university lecturer, they constitute another complete dimension to his thinking. The amount of time managers spend with people in meetings and interviews, unplanned discussions and on the telephone, is a simple recognition of that fact.

People are wholes, not spare parts

Organisations are groups of people out to achieve a limited purpose. You ask people to contribute with *part* of themselves, not their *whole* selves. Therefore there may be a tension between their whole self and the limited part of self you take on.

The manager is to some extent using other people as a means to an end, just as he himself is being used by the shareholders or senior managers as a means to an end. But the first principle in any commonsense morality is that we should treat people as people and all that means.

There are two sets of jagged rocks on either side of a comparatively narrow channel that you have to steer your ship through. On the one side is the old assumption that you are merely hiring 'hands' or 'time', chunks of some impersonal force called 'labour' or 'human resources'. On the other side is the assumption that you have bought the whole person – lock, stock and barrel and that the interests of the individual are co-terminous with the group.

The latter assumption may lead organisations into believing that they can and should mould people by a process of social engineering into 'organisational men', who will think, eat, sleep and dream company business.[4] Here the business organisation is forgetting that its relation with the individual is basically contractual. It is not like belonging to a family, a church or a national community. Of course a person may want to work beyond the call of duty; he may even be said to exploit himself. But that is quite different from the organisation *requiring* you to devote your whole life to its service and demanding the right to pry into your private life or your proper privacy as a person. You are under no obligation to have your opinions monitored or your mind explored.

A corollary is that the employee of whatever rank or status does not have the right to be a whole person at work regardless of the cost or inconvenience to others. The organisation is not there to further self-fulfilment. It is there to achieve its proper purposes. In other words, the concept of a limited contract works both ways.

There is bound to be a *tension* between two ranges or families of values at work – the productivity values (money, goods and services) and the human values. But there need not be a *conflict* – in the sense of open war – between them. Balancing those values is central to the effective management of any organisation.

Consider the views of a young trainee manager who recently graduated in English at Cambridge University.

Many graduates are compelled, indeed are glad, to accept the jobs in business which they are offered. But they remain unwilling to give up at a stroke the personal identities they have wrought through their education.

I would contend that graduates, while accepting jobs in business, do not immediately identify with the values of a business world. That is, they remain profoundly unconvinced of the efficacy of the profit motive as it applies to large corporations.

They retain their belief, albeit romantic, in the opportunity of the individual to express himself; and they remain suspicious of manipulative management techniques. In short, one might say that they feel more one of 'us', than part of 'them'.

Many graduates are now choosing a half-life; by day fulfilling the demands of the executive to the barest minimum, and retreating at nights and weekends to view quite objectively and dispassionately their career 'half'.

This is a quite new managerial schizophrenia which has mingled a private, radical disavowal of a business career with a public acceptance of market necessity, and its full ramifications have yet to be seen.

A senior manager, commenting on these remarks, said, 'Perhaps all students with these expectations should remember that leaving university is only the end of the beginning. This bleating attitude will not earn much sympathy in the business world.' Would that view be closer to your own?

One way to banish this 'managerial schizophrenia' is to create as much overlap as possible between what the organisation wants to do and what the individual wants to do. If that happens, it will be natural for the manager to apply all his brain power to his work. He will strive to become a better decision maker, problem solver and creative thinker because he will, in an important sense, be working for himself as well as serving a common and worthwhile purpose. The sense of alienation, that great foe of good work performance, will give place to a genuine and lasting job satisfaction.

Involving work people in decisions

Should this fuller involvement of the mind in one's work be confined to the manager?

At this point I call attention to the traditional distinction between managers and work people. Generally speaking, it went without saying that managers would feel involved and committed at work because they have to employ their minds to make decisions and solve problems. It was assumed that the workers, as they were known, would not feel so involved, because industry hires only their physical strength or manual dexterity. They are hands not minds. This old distinction needs revising. There is much to be said for the practice of the British construction company Taylor Woodrow. There all – managers, staff and workforce – are referred to simply as team members. The emblem of the company – men pulling together on the same rope – symbolises that positive attitude.

Yet, despite efforts to change it, the traditional attitude to work people still lingers on. It is so deeply entrenched in the collective psyche of managers. Take the following incident, a true story told by a management consultant, as typical.

A wealth of experience and talent on the shopfloor is often ignored by managers.

Some years ago, as a management consultant, I was involved in a major manufacturing project. One important item of continuous production plant proved to be difficult. A team of 'organisation and methods' people failed to solve the problem. Eventually it was decided that I should try. Next morning I introduced myself to the operator, shook his hand, explained the problem and asked him if he had any ideas. He grinned and told me that I was the first person to make this kind of approach. My predecessors had never explained the purpose of their investigation. As I had done him the courtesy of asking his help, he proposed to tell me the answer, giving me the main essentials in two minutes. We had ironed out all the details by lunchtime. I am sure my experience is not unique.

You can probably think of a similar example of the neglect of shopfloor experience and talent at your place of work whether it is office, shop or factory.

Of course it is quite wrong that this activity of eliciting ideas from all employees should be left to management consultants: it is an integral part of what it means to be a business leader today. Here is another example to illustrate this point.

In 1980 it looked as if GEC's high voltage switch gear plant in Stafford would shut down because its main product, a circuit-breaker, was losing money. Two of Lord Weinstock's managers decided to involve the whole workforce. In an empty assembly bay they set out the 503 components of the circuit-breaker, each labelled. Accompanying charts gave a complete breakdown of costs. They invited ideas from everyone. Within a few weeks, 243 ideas were produced from the shopfloor and submitted for analysis to some expert *ad hoc* teams which had been set up for the purpose. The constructive ideas from the workforce accounted for about half of the eventual savings; the manufacturing costs were reduced by one-third and the plant stayed in business. The benefits of asking for help from the shopfloor, however, are more than financial. The convenor of the main trade union at the factory took the view that the exercise 'changed the whole industrial relations climate' in the plant.

In the last resort, whether you see people as your most important resource or as a bloody nuisance depends upon your doctrine of man. For my part I hold the belief that most people, irrespective of colour, creed or race, will respond to a manager's request for suggestions or ideas. For all of us are born helpful. We only become helpless because of what parents or society do to us or if we inherit a particularly unfortunate set of genes. But in general the human race is geared to help one another. That is why man is called a social animal. We could not have survived otherwise.

Our difficulties in drawing out the talents and gifts of people at work are caused by years of inadequate thinking about leadership, communication and decision making, coupled with a failure to teach what there is to learn about them. W.F. Younger, managing director of Hay-MSL management consultants, points to the consequences.

Traditionally, a function of a leader has been to protect his people against the dangers and disadvantages of disruptive change, but much of modern management is concerned with creating and implementing change.

Change in industry has meant mergers, take overs, rationalisation, redundancies, transformation of traditional values and the overthrow of previously accepted pecking orders. Many of the effects have been painful. Managers have been seen as the instruments of this ferment and pain, whilst trade union officials have often emerged in the traditional leadership role of protector in these situations.

However, the likely consequences of industrial change are well researched and recorded, probable reactions of a workforce can be reasonably anticipated. So why has this generation of highly educated managers apparently failed to learn how to inspire its manual and clerical colleagues? Why is there frequently a greater gulf between shopfloor worker and the graduate manager (whose own father may be a blue collar union member) than that which existed between the old autocratic owner manager and his much less priviled employees?

One of the few welcome results of world recession in recent years is that it compelled many managers to take their workforces into their confidence for the first time. Managers have told people the true facts about the financial position, telling them about the competition and what needs to be done to survive and move towards a desired future. It is significant that firms and organisations that have so communicated, that have so shared objectives, that have so identified the problems are those that have forged ahead. In a purposeful climate people are prepared to work all hours to do what needs to be done.

To summarise, most organisations today are people businesses. If nothing else, people are one of their bigger costs. It is essential for enterprises to create within themselves an environment or climate which really stimulates people to use their brains to the maximum. Leadership and good communications are therefore necessary to create those conditions. Then people will produce better corporate decisions, a higher standard of problem solving and much more creative thinking and innovation. Work will be more fun too.

References

1 Stewart, Rosemary, *Managers and their Jobs*, Macmillan, London, 1967.
2 Mintzberg, Henry, *The Nature of Managerial Work*, Harper & Row, New York, 1973.
3 Dixon, Norman, *On the Psychology of Military Incompetence*, Futura, London, 1979.
4 Whyte, William H., *The Organisational Man,* Simon & Schuster, New York, 1955; Jonathan Cape, London, 1957.

2 Know your mind

You can start to improve your decision making ability by sharpening the thinking tools which nature and education have provided. Chapter 2 offers a sketchmap of how your mind – and the minds of every employee in your organisation – actually works. Then we shall consider the main components, so to speak, of the.model. To become more effective as a thinker it is necessary to separate out and sharpen up the major mental abilities – which in acts of decision making or problem solving – are so virtually inseparable.

Understanding how your mind works when it is thinking about a decision or problem is not easy; it is like trying to jump on your shadow. Most managers are not introspective by nature but that is no barrier to becoming more aware of the range and depth of your basic mental functions. The secret is not solitary introspection, which may merely make you introverted, but to catch your mind off-guard when it is doing its business.

Your mental functions are like a football team before the

camera anxious to pose for you, arms folded and faces smiling, perhaps with a silver cup or two at their feet. But that kind of photography session tells you nothing about their footballing skills or indeed the game of football itself. You have to see them struggling against another team, passing the ball from one to the other, giving ground and then surging forwards, obeying rules and breaking them, to come near to understanding what football is all about.

Try the following exercise. It calls into play some important mental functions.

Who Is Going to Barker Street?

Five taxi-drivers have been summoned to pick up five fares at a London club. On arrival, they find that their passengers are slightly intoxicated. Each man has a different first and last name, a different profession, a different destination; and each man's wife has a different first name.

Unable to determine who's who and who's going where, the taxi-drivers ask you to find out: **Who is the baker? What is Bert's last name? Who is going to Barker Street?** You collect these facts from the passengers:

1 Brad is married to Betty.
2 Barbara's husband gets into the third taxi.
3 Bart is a banker.
4 The last taxi goes to Barton Street.
5 Beatrice lives in Burton Street.
6 The butcher gets into the fourth taxi.
7 Bob gets into the second taxi.
8 Bernice is married to the broker.
9 Mr Barker lives in Burton Street.
10 Mr Burger gets into the taxi in front of Brenda's husband.
11 Mr Bunger gets into the first taxi.
12 Mr Baker lives in Burbon Street.
13 The barber lives in Baker Street.
14 Mr Baker gets into the taxi in front of Mr Burke.
15 The barber is three taxis in front of Brian.
16 Mr Burger is in the taxi in front of the butcher.

If you have completed the exercise successfully in 20 minutes you have done well; 30 minutes is average, while 15 minutes or less is exceptionally good. Check your answers by turning to page 166. No peeping allowed!

Brain power

When working on the above exercise you were deploying a formidable amount of brain power. Your brain contains around 10,000,000,000 nerve cells or neurons. According to some scientists, you lose about 10,000 brains cells a day, but so great is your natural supply that, at 80 years of age, you will only have lost about 3 per cent of your brain capacity. If you sat down and counted each brain cell in your head, at the rate of one a second, you would still be counting in 30,000 years time.

Each neuron looks like a tiny starfish or octopus, with synapses – places where nerve cells join – lining the feelers. Each cell is capable of linking up with about 10,000 of its neighbours. That gives you an astronomical figure of possible combinations: 1 followed by 10 million kilometres of standard typewritten noughts. The number of possible connections in a single brain, to put it another way, is larger than the number of atoms presumed to exist in the entire universe. Chemical reactions involving somewhere between 100,000 and about one million cells were going on in your head at any given moment as you tackled that problem of who goes to Barker Street.

The difference between *brain* and *mind* can be easily illustrated by reference to a television set. If you open up the back – all those coloured wires and circuits – you are in the realm of brain research. The neurosurgeon is like the electrician who can repair the set. If you look at the screen of the television, however, you are in the realm of mind. It has the dimension of meaning. The workings of mind, rather than the brain as such, is of course the central concern in this book.

What brain research suggests, however, is that our minds have almost limitless potential. Your brain is much better than you think it is. Most of the problems we have in thinking are not because of any fundamental shortcomings in this biological super computer but because we do not know how to use it effectively.

Three families of abilities

The mind has several different ways of working and they can be called families of abilities. The exercise above obviously required you to use your *analytical* abilities as a thinker, and also to think *logically*, which is a near relation to analysing. So two members at least of the most prominent family of thinking ability – the *analysers* – were hard at work. But they are not the only family which works in the busy offices of the mind. The three chief clans are:

- *The analysers*
  The prime ability here is to separate a whole into its component parts. The analysers are like ants. They can resolve anything complex into its simple elements. The word itself comes from the old Greek verb meaning to unloosen or to break up.
- *The synthesisers*
  The central ability here is the reverse one to analysing, namely to think and form wholes. Components or parts are assembled together. The Greek word behind our one means to piece together. (Synthesising may not be the best name for this clan, but it is the nearest I can get).
- *The valuers*
  The valuers revolve around the perception of value, worth or significance. They include all forms of judging, criticising and evaluating. Their relatives do the actual measuring and counting and testing, work which the valuers often regard as beneath their dignity.

Each of these clans is the subject of following chapters, so I shall not pause to illustrate them further now. But you may like to reflect further about them for a few moments and try to decide in which of the three kinds of ability are your strongest and weakest.

Using your depth mind

The *depth mind* is an unfamiliar phrase to most people. I have coined it to stand for those unconscious and subconscious parts of our mind which actually work for us. It has been derived by analogy with the sea: the three families we have been looking at are abilities of the conscious mind that goes on upon the surface;

the *subconscious* is the depth of a few fathoms where the light penetrates, while the *unconscious* is the deeper recesses into which we cannot see.

One vital contribution to our thinking by the depth mind is our memory. One of the mysteries of the mind is how we can recall things so swiftly on demand. If you are asked a fact, such as someone's name, you may often say (if you are like me) 'Give me a minute or two and I'll remember it'. A few minutes later the name pops into your conscious mind. Amazing.

Memory in its various forms as our private data bank plays a central part in our thinking, but it is not the only contribution of the depth mind to effective mental activity. Following popular versions of Freud, who did more than anyone else to put the unconscious mind on the map, we tend to conceive of the unconscious as a kind of dustbin for our early sexual frustrations. Into it drops all our mental rubbish – the bruised egos, the damaged wishes, the broken loves, the resentments, fears, hatreds and rages of our childhood. We then force down the lid on these suppressed feelings. But they erupt again in our dreams and in various forms of behaviour, such as the celebrated 'Freudian slips'. We have to remember, however, that Freud based his conclusions upon the study of mentally ill patients.

To counter this rather negative image of the unconscious, the later Freudian psychologists felt it necessary to coin yet another word – the *preconscious*. This stands for the realm where helpful subliminal thinking takes place, and is roughly equivalent to my own term, the depth mind.

The most interesting manifestation of this more helpful depth mind work is what we often call creative thinking. No one knows quite how the depth mind goes about its work. We do know, however, that it is capable of *synthesising* apparently unrelated pieces into quite complicated jig-saw puzzles of meaning.

Robert Louis Stevenson described his own methods in imaginative work in this way. 'Unconscious thought, there is the only method: macerate your subject, let it boil slow, then take the lid off and look in – and there your stuff is, good or bad'.

The depth mind can supply you with the seed of an idea and carry out an often intricate process of synthesis for you over a period of time. Both contributions are present in this passage by Lewis Carroll:

I was walking on a hillside, alone, one bright summer day, when suddenly there came into my head one line of verse – one solitary line – 'For the Snark was a Boojum, you see'. I knew not what it meant, then: I know not what it means, now: but I wrote it down: and, some time afterwards, the rest of the stanza occurred to me, that being its last line: and so by degrees, at moments during the next year or two, the rest of the poem pieced itself together . . .

I suggest that the depth of mind can also *analyse* and *value*. In the former respect it can be compared to your stomach, which is fed with powerful enzymes which can take to bits the meals you commit to it. The analogy of digestion, the process of making food absorbable by dissolving it and breaking it down into simpler chemical compounds, seems especially apt.

With regard to valuing it is again impossible to be precise about what goes on. What is clear is that our values inhabit our deeper minds and are often obscure to ourselves until we do something or have to choose between two alternatives. Rationally we may believe (quite rightly) that decisions should be made on the basis of our values. It is often the case however that the decision comes first and then it tells us something about what our values really are. There is another related phenomenon, namely that the act of decision somehow confers value – 'Because I have chosen Smith as branch manager therefore he must be good'.

You may have had the experience of 'sleeping on' some decision or problem and finding that your mind has made up itself next morning. If you haven't give it a try. The depth mind principle can also be used to memorise material. Just before you go to sleep read what you have to learn, preferably out loud, and as you settle down concentrate on the material. As soon as you wake try to recall what you read – you may be surprised at how much you have remembered.

Can you develop this immense reserve power of your depth mind? Yes, within reason. Some people are more gifted in that way than others. But *awareness* of the part played by the subconscious, coupled with *friendly interest* in how it works, can set you on the path to self development. You will find more specific suggestions later in the book.

Managing emotion

Thinking and emotion or feeling are often contrasted. But the mind is one. It is not surprising therefore that there is a complex relationship between thinking and emotion. It is important for anyone who wishes to manage their thinking to understand this relationship.

Emotion and motive both concern that which moves you. Emotion is the partly mental, partly physical response of being stirred up by someone or something. Physical danger or threat, as we have seen, produces a stirring up of emotion: strong feelings of fear and physiological changes that prepare your body for immediate vigorous action. If prolonged, such experiences may add up to stress.

Emotion carries a stronger implication of excitement or agitation than feeling, which suggests that our most powerful emotions lie dormant in the depths of our minds and are only stirred up on rare occasions. It is helpful to think of emotion in terms of the weather. Emotions are rather like strong winds, raging thunderstorms or blazing heat, while feelings are breezes, showers and the warmth of sun on the skin.

As we know, feelings and emotions accompany thinking. An apparently simple problem which resists repeated attempts at solving it will induce the feelings of frustration. Thinking can be painful and it can be pleasurable. Indeed it can be so pleasurable that it becomes addictive. There are managers (often those who habitually attend seminars and conferences on general topics) who are completely hooked on the hedonistic pleasures of thinking. As decision means an end to thinking and the beginning of action, they tend to resist that evil hour by always finding an excuse for more talk. At the other extreme are the managers who find that thinking hurts in the sense of giving them a physical headache or being just unpleasant. Therefore they avoid it.

There is one practical point about emotions. Highly creative people report something which has been called *the hedonic response*. It is the feeling of being on the right track. If you like, it is an advance payment of emotional rewards of success. Sometimes, then, our emotions refuse to adopt the role of 'full supporting cast'. They become pioneers or scouts reporting back to us that we are making progress even though the rational faculties of the mind are still in the dark.

Roadblocks to learning

One aspect of emotion touches upon your success or failure in studying this book, so I must deal with it now – the fear of the difficult. As such it is one of the hydra-heads of that monster Fear which slumbers in the capacious caves of our unconscious minds. In his inaugural address on 4 March 1933, as the world slid further into Depression, President Roosevelt told the American nation in ringing tones: 'Let me assert my firm belief that the only thing we have to fear is fear itself'. There is no better motto for a thinker.

Take languages. 'Learning French is too difficult for my poor brain', said an export manager to me. He is wrong. His brain could do it – he cannot. One Victorian linguist was able to speak 200 languages. It is possible to know a vocabulary of about 800,000 words in English, but most of us operate with far fewer than 20,000 words. Such remarkable feats pose a key question. If such brains differ only a little from our own, what spare capacity for learning does the average person waste? Either he is afraid of the mental effort involved, or possibly he has tried it before and been unsuccessful – through not trying hard enough or indeed because of the wrong kind of instruction. He may have been taught by a poor teacher whom he loathed.

Take science as another example. Sir Herman Bondi, FRS, the Chief Scientist to the Department of Energy, said recently that one consequence of Einstein's great popularity as a person was that theoretical physics was wrongly believed to be unintelligible to all but a few specialists. 'To regard theoretical physics as more difficult than, for example, learning a foreign language is, I consider, unjustifiable and a great pity', said Bondi. 'If I were to offer a man ten thousand pounds to learn Albanian, he would say, "It will be difficult but I can do it". If I were to offer him the same sum to learn theoretical physics, he would say, "I cannot do it. I haven't the right sort of mind".'

Conclusion

You should now understand how the human mind works when it is thinking to some purpose. You should have identified the principal skills which have to be developed. You may also have begun to form some picture of your personal mental profile. Where are your strengths and weaknesses as a thinker?

This chapter should also have changed your attitude to those who work with you or under you. Everyone else in the workforce has 10,000,000,000 brain cells like you. Employing such formidable minds probably constitutes the organisation's highest cost. What are the implications of those facts for you as a manager and also for your organisation? Surely that you should do all in your power to harness the brain power of every team member to the task in hand.

3 Analysing

In managing any aspect of a business possession of a good analytical mind is essential. This chapter describes further the purpose or role of analysis in thinking. By the end you should have a fuller understanding of analytical ability and a working idea of how good you are at it. Competent analysing is especially important to you because of its chief effect, which is clarity of thought.

Figure 3.1 shows the 25 attributes referred to on p. 2 listed in the order of value for their own work assigned to them by 120 executive heads of Britain's largest private and public industrial organisations. Now put two marks on a scale of 0 to 10 beside them expressing the degree to which, in your opinion, practical and professional experience develops them in contrast to academic work and examinations. For example, if you think *astuteness* is overwhelmingly developed by academic work you may give it a mark of 9 out of 10 in the academic box and 0 out of 10 in the professional experience box.

Ranking of attributes most valuable at the top level of management	Attribute developed mainly by academic work	Attribute developed mainly by professional work
1 Ability to take decisions	☐	☐
2 Leadership	☐	☐
3 Integrity	☐	☐
4 Enthusiasm	☐	☐
5 Imagination	☐	☐
6 Willingness to work hard	☐	☐
7 Analytical ability	☐	☐
8 Understanding of others	☐	☐
9 Ability to spot opportunities	☐	☐
10 Ability to meet unpleasant situations	☐	☐
11 Ability to adapt quickly to change	☐	☐
12 Willingness to take risks	☐	☐
13 Enterprise	☐	☐
14 Capacity to speak lucidly	☐	☐
15 Astuteness	☐	☐
16 Ability to administer efficiently	☐	☐
17 Open-mindedness	☐	☐
18 Ability to 'stick it'	☐	☐
19 Willingness to work long hours	☐	☐
20 Ambition	☐	☐
21 Single-mindedness	☐	☐
22 Capacity for lucid writing	☐	☐
23 Curiosity	☐	☐
24 Skill with numbers	☐	☐
25 Capacity for abstract thought	☐	☐

Figure 3.1

Having checked your answers against those of the chief executives (p. 168) you will notice that *analytical ability* is high on the list of most valuable attributes at number seven. But the chief executives believed that professional experience alone played only a small part in developing it. Do you agree with that conclusion?

Incidentally, the chief executives in the survey placed weight on passing examinations at school, college or university, but more as a test of character than of intelligence. In the case of professional qualifications they were valued as giving precise information about whether or not a man has the particular knowledge needed for a particular job. The managing director of Consolidated Gold Fields made an interesting point: 'I attach more importance to the qualifications a man has obtained *in his own time* than to those he has obtained by staying on at university'. But it fell to a member of a control group of 66 novelists and poets, John Wain, to give the most eloquent defence of examinations as tests of personality and character: 'To be successful in examinations of any kind means self-discipline, capacity to do unpalatable work, ability to concentrate and willingness to think about something other than yourself – all useful in any kind of situation and for any kind of person'.

Academic work does shape and examinations do test or reveal our natural ability to think analytically. But there are plenty of examples of men, such as Henry Ford and Roy Thomson, who left school at 14 years old, and yet developed an excellent if narrow analytical ability. Natural aptitude plus a good education plus experience is, as always, a winning combination.

Identifying the hallmarks of a good analytical mind

How do you spot a good analytical mind in a subordinate or in someone applying for a job? First, we have to define what we mean by analytical ability.

Many people think of analysis as simply taking things to bits, like a child dismantling a toy. But it is much more than that – you are looking for something. What your quarry actually is will depend on the nature of the case, but you may be:

31

- establishing the *relations* of the parts to each other and to the whole
- finding the true *cause* or causes of the problem
- identifying the *issue* at stake, the 'either–or' upon which a decision must rest (what a good trial judge does)
- discovering a *law* in nature
- searching for the *principles* behind experience

These general points can be illustrated by examples drawn from particular fields, as shown in Table 3.1.

The analysing achievements of scientific research are often spectacular. Incidentally, it is encouraging for many of us to reflect that success in examinations, like early precocity, is an unreliable guide to intellectual ability: a survey of Fellows of the Royal Society has shown that many of them possess only mediocre degrees.

Table 3.1

FIELDS	ACTIVITY
Chemistry	The resolution of a chemical compound into its elements and any foreign substances it may contain
Optics	The resolution of light into its prismatic constituents
Literature	The critical examination of any production, so as to exhibit its elements in simple form
Grammar	Determining the elements composing a sentence or part of it
Mathematics	The resolving of problems by reducing them to equations
Philosophy	Resolving complex expressions into simpler or more basic ones

Take one achievement in the field of biochemistry – the chemistry of life. The building blocks of virtually all life – from bacteria to humans – are cells. The nature and tasks of each cell are determined by its genes. The genes are long chains of the chemical called DNA, the famous 'double helix'. Each chain has only four types of 'link' (in fact, four chemical groups), but the links can be strung together in an almost infinite number of different sequences. The instructions which tell each cell how to reproduce itself lie in the exact sequence of those links. The formula above charts the sequence of links in one of the simplest forms of life – a virus only one-millionth of an inch across. As a computer printout, this formula is 50 feet long. A comparable printout for the genes bearing the instructions to make a human being would stretch 10,000 miles, or almost halfway round the earth. It is for working out a way of charting these sequences – the code of life – that Dr Frederick Sanger of the Medical Research Council was awarded his second Nobel Prize in 1980.

Ten thousand million viruses could occupy the space within this asterisk ✳ , each with a gene chain which would take four pages of computer printout to chart it. Sanger analysed just one virus, Phi-X-174, into its 5,386 sub-units. Over the years Sanger has improved his analytical techniques dramatically. At the beginning it took him a year to chart 50 of the sub-units of such a virus. Today it is possible to map up to 1,000 sub-units a day.

Sanger attempted to map the sequence of the twenty amino-acids which are sub-units of the protein insulin. It turned out to be a fortunate choice: as proteins go, insulin is a comparatively small molecule. Even so, sequencing a protein was so formidable an undertaking that no more than a couple of points in a chain had ever been determined before. Sanger had to develop chemical analysis techniques from scratch; and even identifying the easiest links – the amino acids at the ends of the chain – occupied months. It took him ten years to work out the complete structure.

To carry through, almost single-handed, a research project of this length, with all its inevitable frustrations and setbacks, requires staying power of a high order. It is a quality Sanger possessed in abundance. 'I am', he said, 'very strongly self-motivated'.

Sanger's story shows us that analytical ability by itself,

together with the capacity to develop and employ advanced analytical techniques, is not enough for real achievement as a thinker: you need flair or luck, perseverance and considerable self-motivation as well.

Analytical ability in management

Analysing plays a central part in problem solving. The sifting process of separating facts from opinions or suppositions, pulling the elements of the problem apart, are happening as you work your way towards the heart of the problem. Your mind has to work like a shoal of piranha fish, stripping the problem down to its essentials.

A less common form of analysis in a manager is the ability to think for himself from first principles. The hallmarks of a mind of this kind are simplicity, originality, coupled with great clarity. Dimitro Comino, the founder of Dexion Ltd., once told me: 'I have to spend a lot of time making things clear to myself. I go back to basic principles, but then they are so obvious that no one is interested'.

The Case of the Careless Consultant

Consulting is a profession that calls for a high order of analytical skills, whether the consultant is in medicine, technology or business. There was once a company that sold iron bedsteads the length and breadth of Britain. In spite of many actions, sales were falling. So a consultant was hired to identify the cause. He knew about analysis and fact gathering so he collected detailed statistics relating to the salesforce – number of salesmen, number of customers, miles travelled, calls made, commission earned and so forth. He concluded that the salespeople in Scotland and Wales were less effective than those in England and recommended they be replaced. Soon it became obvious that the new salesmen fared no better than their predecessors. The problem had nothing to do with the quality of the salesforce. The root cause of the company's difficulty lay in the market place: iron bedsteads were going out of fashion.

This consultant was rather like a medical counterpart trying to cure a painful foot by amputating it. That solves the apparent problem. But it is a rather drastic action for a badly fitting shoe.

Apart from analysing problems when they occur, do you set aside time to analyse what is going on in your own field to determine the underlying simple principles? Too much of this kind of activity probably leads to neglect of normal workload, but now and again it is very helpful.

You may question why a person who thinks quickly from first principles should be deemed original. But our education does not train us to do that. We are lumbered with a mass of secondary or derived knowledge, most of which will soon be out-of-date. Our desire to conform socially and mentally with each other also militates against such clear thinking. We are not taught to think for ourselves. You may recall the horrified reaction of Shelley's mother when discussing her boy's future education:

Friend	'Oh, send him somewhere where they will teach him to think for himself'.
Mrs Shelley	'Teach him to think for himself? Oh, my God, teach him rather to think like other people'.

"There's a limit to the decisions a top executive can make in one day, you know."

35

The skill of asking yourself questions

Thinking involves asking questions and endeavouring to find answers to these questions. By 'asking questions' I do not mean all interrogative sentences. Some questions are merely rhetorical. A genuine question demands an answer. To be thinking hard about something is to be in a questioning frame of mind. In order to get into that state you need to be puzzled about something. What we are puzzled about may be how to start the car engine; or it may be how to make a million pounds by a certain date, or how best to learn Japanese. We may be puzzled about who to promote, or why globules of air gather in sheet glass when it is being manufactured in a certain way.

The original question should then lead to a host of analytical questions, the piranha fish of the mind. These will be addressed to ourselves and to other people in an attempt to strip the matter down to the bare bones. Textbooks on decision making and problem solving usually supply long checklists of such questions but this should not be necessary if you have grasped the principle of articulating questions. It helps sometimes to speak them aloud and listen to your own questions, or to write them down.

In the early days you can borrow questions from other people, such as 'when did the problem first arise'? But you should, with practice, be able to develop your own portfolio of analytical questions to bring to any problem or situation. They are your mental tools or spanners. Some of them, you will find, fit a much wider range of situation than others. Go back to those magic words: Who? Which? Why? (and Why not?) When? Where? and How?

Analysing is such a basic part of our mental equipment that we tend to take it for granted. We forget that it can become limited in range and blunted at the edge. You should aim to take a greater pride in your analytical ability and develop it whenever you see a feasible opportunity for so doing.

The analytical methods of logicians

The logician is especially concerned with what can be properly concluded from statements or propositions. In formal logic a set of two or more propositions and a conclusion is called a syllogism. Here is an example:

> All coins are round (major premise)
> You have a coin in your pocket (minor premise)
> Your coin is round (conclusion)

The relationship between the premises and the conclusion, or what they entail, is often called the inference.

The fact that academic logicians use these rather trivial-looking examples and that they tend to emphasise the formal relationship between statements should not blind us to the fact that they are struggling with a central theme in all our quests for truth, namely *the relation of the general to the particular.* In the real world we sometimes think in syllogisms without being aware of it.

One result of disciplining your mind to logical thinking is a greater awareness of the part that premises play, especially the kind that are generalisations. You will have noticed that the major premise above is false: all coins are *not* round. Therefore the argument based upon it collapses like a pack of cards.

The danger of holding a large stock of unsubstantiated generalisations in your mind is that you might start using them as premises. 'No, Miss Jones, I cannot offer you a manager's job in the finance department. For one thing, women just can't count, they aren't really numerate, you know. Also, I should have to send you on an expensive course, and all women leave to have babies just when they are fully trained. I expect you'll report me to the Equal Opportunities Commission – all malicious women do – but I promise you that they will not find me prejudiced. I pride myself on having an open mind'.

To summarise: what goes wrong in reasoning or argument can usually be traced to unsound premises or faulty logical steps. More often than not the reasoning is sound, it is the premises that must be examined.

Before moving on from formal logic there are two further lessons to be learnt by the manager. The first stems from a study of how logicians go about analysing arguments, and the second is a useful summary of two directions in thinking, called inductive and deductive reasoning.

Filleting arguments

A good fishmonger can fillet a fish for you in a few seconds so that you see the hard, bony skeleton. It is a useful skill for a thinker. The logicians do it by reducing arguments to a form of simple algebra. It is then possible to detect error much more easily.

> If Jones was an outstanding manager he would be promoted to the board.
> He has been made a director.
> Therefore, Jones is an outstanding manager.

This fallacious mode of argument is soon revealed by its skeleton:

> If A, then B,
> B
> Therefore A.

Of course it is quite possible that Jones is an outstanding manager, but that conclusion is not a necessary inference from the reasoning offered. If we know it, we know it on other grounds.

Logical reasoning, then, centres upon what may or may not be properly concluded or inferred. It can be called consecutive thinking because it is concerned with thinking in steps, the last one not being immediately apparent when you first embark on the journey. Algebra or mathematics method is therefore essentially logical, with letters or numbers in place of words as its elements.

Two other terms from the realm of logic are worth knowing: *inductive* and *deductive*. They are both ways of inferring things. Deduction means drawing a particular inference from a general proposition, while induction is the opposite: forming a generalisation by considering a number of particular instances. The latter used to be regarded as the core of scientific method. Research activities – whatever the kind – provide good examples of induction. It would be an instance of deduction if we said: 'All salesmen like fast cars. Fred does not like fast cars and therefore he is no salesman'. The conclusion, of course, is invalid in this case. A correct deduction is present in the following syllogism: 'All ordinary shareholders are entitled to vote at the annual general meeting. All the directors are shareholders. Therefore, all directors are entitled to vote at the annual general meeting'.

Lewis Carroll produced some wonderful examples of arguments in deducting logic, including this: 'No one takes in *The Times* unless he is well educated. No hedgehogs can read. Those who cannot read are not well educated. Therefore, no hedgehog takes in *The Times*'.

In contrast to this kind of thinking, inductive logic at work can be seen in such things as test marketing where a new or modified product is sold in a very small part of a company's market to see if it has any 'customer appeal'. The reasoning here follows this line: 'The new product sells very well in the North-east and the South-west. There is no reason why it should not sell well nationally'.

Other examples of this kind of reasoning include product development, opinion surveys, market research and all the work that goes on in all the laboratories around the world. The aim is to make a prediction about the behaviour of everything or everybody in a particular class, by studying a small sample of that class.

In summary, logical thinking in the sense of being able *to draw proper conclusions from information or evidence* (as contrasted to general or particular premises of a lecture room nature), is central to most professions, from car mechanics to police detectives. That ability is vital to managers as well. Do you possess it?

Exercises in logical thinking

You have already had one attempt at logical thinking (on p. 21). Armed with that experience and the knowledge in this chapter – together with a piece of paper and pencil – you should not have too much difficulty with the following games. The answers are on p. 169 and the time allowed for them together is 10–15 minutes providing you have not seen any of the problems before.

Each of three friends – Mr Carpenter, Mr Mason and Mr Painter – is engaged in a different occupation. By a strange coincidence, one is a carpenter, one a mason and one a painter; but their names do not necessarily match their trades.

Assuming that only one of the following four statements is true, can you work out who does what?

Mr Carpenter is not a painter
Mr Mason is not a carpenter
Mr Carpenter is a carpenter
Mr Mason is not a painter

● A logician with some time to kill in a small town decided to have his hair cut. The town had only two barbers, each with his own shop. The logician glanced into one shop and saw that it was extremely untidy. The barber needed a shave, his clothes were unkempt, his hair was badly cut. The other shop was extremely neat. The barber was freshly shaved and spotlessly dressed, his hair neatly trimmed. The logician returned to the first shop for his haircut. Why?

● 'I guarantee,' said the pet-shop salesman, 'that this parrot will repeat every word it hears.' A customer bought the parrot but found it would not speak a single word. Nevertheless, the salesman told the truth. Can you explain?

● In a certain African village there live 800 women. Three per cent of them are wearing one ear-ring. Of the other 97 per cent, half are wearing two ear-rings, half are wearing none. How many ear-rings altogether are being worn by the women?

● Two trains are 100 miles apart. They are moving towards each other, one at 40 mph, the other at 60 mph. A plane flying backwards and forwards between the two trains is travelling at 80 mph. How far does the plane fly before the trains meet?

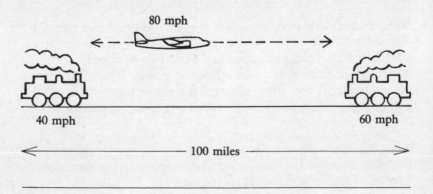

Think backwards

Often the desired end is clear: the problem is simply to get there. Use your imagination to visualise that end state, and then work *backwards* step-by-step using the logical method. This can be called *future perfect* thinking – when an event yet to happen is treated as if it was over.

Think it out (1)

Two girls and a woman wish to sail to an island. Their boat holds either the two girls or the woman. If all are competent sailors, how can they get to the island in as few trips as possible?

Visualise that end state. If you work backwards from that first trip, you begin to see that someone must bring the boat back from the island. Thus the two girls must sail over. One girl will remain on the island while the other sails the boat back. And the rest of the problem simply requires keeping track of where everyone is at a given time.

Think it out (2)

Now you have grasped the principle, apply it to solve this similar problem:

Martha has to get her two babies, Sara and Roger, as well as the family cat, out to the car. Because Martha has a broken arm, she can carry only one baby or the cat at a time.

Unfortunately, neither child can be left alone with the cat. Sara pulls the cat's tail, causing general havoc, and the cat sheds fur on Roger's brown clothes. How does she get everyone to the car in as few trips as possible?

The answer to this problem is on p. 169.

Organise the facts

A logical approach is inseparable from re-arranging the information available. A problem is often a jumble of information which needs to be:

- separated into its component parts
- re-arranged or restructured

A problem is often a solution in disguise.

As you will have discovered when you tackled the exercise on p. 21 making charts or matrixes – a branch of thinking visually with your pen as a tool, rather than in your head – is a vital supporting strategy.

Think it out (3)

Anne, Heather and Theresa live next door to each other. Heather has the flat in the middle. They work as a chemist, a radio announcer and a doctor, but not necessarily in that order. The announcer walks Theresa's dog when Theresa goes away on holiday. The chemist taps on Anne's wall when Anne's stereo is too loud. What career does each woman have?

Try sorting out the given information in a systematic way. Make a chart to spell out every option and look for clues with which to eliminate the options one at a time. If the announcer walks Theresa's dog, then Theresa is not the announcer. The chemist taps on Anne's wall, indicating that Anne is not the chemist. So cross out those possibilities.

Re-read the problem to find less obvious clues and implications. The chemist – since it isn't Anne – must be either Heather or Theresa. But Theresa cannot tap on Anne's wall – Heather's flat is in the middle. So Heather must be the chemist. Theresa, since she is neither the radio announcer nor the chemist, can only be the doctor. Anne must therefore be the radio announcer.

Think it out (4)

In a plane flying to London, five passengers are seated in a row next to each other. Their professions are journalist, singer, teacher, naval captain and engineer. They are of the following nationalities: English, French, German, Italian, Dutch. They are various ages (21, 24, 32, 40 and 52). The passengers take part in various sports (handball, swimming, volleyball, athletics and football). Their destinations in England are London, Birmingham, Manchester, Newcastle and Plymouth.

1 The engineer is seated on the extreme left.
2 The volleyball player is seated in the middle.
3 The Englishman is a journalist.
4 The singer is 21.
5 The teacher's sport is swimming.
6 The naval captain is travelling to Plymouth.
7 The handball player is French.
8 The passenger from Holland is bound for Birmingham.
9 The passenger bound for London is 32 years old.
10 The athlete is bound for Newcastle.
11 The passenger from France is seated next to the German.
12 The 40-year-old passenger is seated next to the passenger who is bound for Manchester.
13 The 24-year-old passenger is seated next to the passenger who is travelling to Birmingham.
14 The engineer is seated next to the Italian.
15 The passenger on the extreme right is older than the passenger from Holland.

How old is the Naval Captain?
What is the nationality of the football player?
(Time allowed: 20 minutes)
See p. 169 for the answer.

The logic of the situation

Most situations which require an answer or a decision have a form of logic in them. This bears some relation to the logic of the philosophers, but it is a rather different sort of animal and much more recognisable to managers.

Logic in this sense is the inevitable or predictable consequence when you add up the factors in a situation. If you are in a motorcar speeding at one hundred miles per hour and you hit another car travelling at the same speed, the logic of the situation is that you are going to be killed or very seriously injured.

Appealing to the logic of the situation is pointing to something that forces a decision apart from, or even in opposition to, your own or other people's inclinations. The logic of war, for example, might compel you as a general to burn a town or shell a city.

Because logic in this sense can be used to justify such extraordinary actions it is important to subject these kinds of arguments to an especially searching scrutiny. The logic of physical laws, such as gravity or motion, is in a different class to the logic derived from so-called economic, social and psychological laws. You should distinguish between empirical observations of cause-and-effect, which gives you a sense of the logic of situations, and reasoning from theories about general situations, which is a different and more academic kind of logic.

In summary, logical thinking is only a small part of effective thinking. It is a main branch of the analysing family, with an established and respectable offspring in the mathematical and physical sciences. But there are occasions when you have to think logically as a manager, either deductively or inductively. You will certainly need to draw the proper logical conclusions from situations. Be able to reason by steps down a logical path when that sort of thinking is needed. It is an important route to the truth.

At this point you have an option. You can either tackle another game in analytical and logical thinking, *The Missing Missile,* or you can move on to Chapter 4. If you have taken more than ten minutes on the exercise in this chapter I recommend you choose the first option.

The Missing Missile

This exercise is designed to test your ability to cut through waffle and reach the nub of the matter. What is essential information and what is not? Then you have to decide upon your priorities. What is important and what is not? What is possible and what is not? In other words, you must analyse the situation and decide how you are going to handle it.

Activity

Put your plan for solving this problem on paper, giving your reasons, before checking against my answer on p. 171. You should complete the game in thirty minutes.

You are one of a small group of young officers, who are proceeding to the West Indies on an adventure training exercise, and have decided to make your own way by cargo boat. You are using some of your annual leave, and have applied to the Ministry of Defence for part of the cost of your passage. At 08.30 hrs, some days out of port and after some very rough weather, you are enjoying a walk on deck when you notice that the ship has suddenly changed course. You have hardly noted this when you are asked to go at once to the Captain's cabin where you find the Captain, his radio operator and your seven brother officers. The Captain speaks as follows:

'Gentlemen, my Radio Officer has just brought me a message – a FLASH signal from the authorities at Cape Kennedy requesting immediate assistance. Before you ask any questions let me tell you that the request has Ministry of Defence approval; and now to give you the details.

A new, secret rocket, containing a special nose cone, was fired from Cape Kennedy a short while ago. Initially it behaved well, then deviated, and efforts to destroy it by radio signals failing, it continued its flight, but on a new course. The experts cannot understand this and say that it is impossible unless another control has taken over. They have no other controls operating, which implies that an unfriendly state by means of instruments in a very high altitude aircraft, submarine, or elsewhere, has been able to redirect the flight of the rocket. Whatever the system, the rocket has now landed, but not at its correct destination.

Its signals lasted long enough for the experts to pick up its direction, and, with its known fuel range, they are satisfied that it has landed on an uninhabited island less than 70 miles from our present position. My chart shows that the island is quite small and shaped rather like a shoe with its toe pointing westwards. It has a rocky coastline, with sandbanks or reefs running out in some places as much as 7 miles, except on the NORTH EAST coast, which, however, has steep cliffs and high ground up to 1500 ft.

Now to the main point; you have been ordered to find the cone and to ensure its safety at all costs until 09.00 hrs tomorrow, when US forces will arrive and take over responsibility. The cone is approx 9 ft high and 2 ft in diameter at the base, painted yellow with 2 luminous patches four feet square. It is not radio-active.

I have altered course, the ship is going at full speed and we shall arrive off the island in under six hours. Now, Gentlemen, the rest is up to you'.

In reply to questions the Captain answers

'I can give you two small boats, without engines, each with ample room for six people and three cwt of stores. We have sufficient oars but with the present sea, no small boat will make more than 2 mph, and that will be hard work. Swimming, even for a powerful swimmer, will be quite out of the question for the next 36 hours. Yes, you can have as much food and water and clothing as you want. We have equipment such as compasses, cooking utensils and torches etc., but there are only eight torch batteries each with three hours of reasonable life. The only cover I can offer you against possible bad weather are a couple of bell tents, rather old-fashioned and heavy, but in good condition and absolutely waterproof. From the ship's armoury you can take .38 pistols, a verey pistol, shot guns, and as much ammunition as you think you will require.

My Radio Officer and I are the only two British members of the ship's company, and because of the security risk you cannot take anyone else, but I regret that neither of us can be spared from our duties.

Here is a sketch map prepared from my chart which you may keep and which I hope will be useful to you. I must point out that the contours, which, as you know, are drawn at vertical intervals at specific heights above sea-level, have, in this sketch, been shown at vertical intervals of 250 ft. The island consists of volcanic rock, and, because of its rough and uneven surface, is likely to be hard going except along the south coast where there is level ground'.

With the other officers you leave the cabin and go to the dining room to study and discuss the problem. Half-an-hour later the Captain joins you and says that he has received the following further information.

'A small unidentified submarine, not of the NATO forces, has been reported south of the island, moving north. It submerged quickly on being seen, but, if it continues on its present course, should arrive off the island at sunset. There are only three known areas along the coast where even a small boat could land, but from one of them runs a channel which would enable a submarine to get within 400 yards of the beach. This is off the north east coast; elsewhere a submarine would have to lie off two miles. Next, the experts have produced the following data, as a result of rechecking their calculations in an endeavour to pin-point the area of the cone. The cone is lying in the south east area of the island, some 300–400 ft above sea-level, about one and a half miles inland and on a slope which faces west. They apologise for not doing better, but say that this information can be accepted as accurate. You will

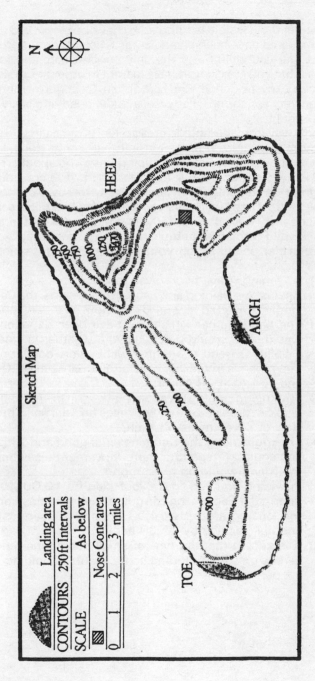

Sketch Map

N

HEEL

ARCH

TOE

Landing area
CONTOURS 250ft Intervals
As below
Nose Cone area
SCALE
0   1   2   3 miles

1250
1000
500
750

250
500

500

47

observe that the possible landing areas have been marked on the sketch map and have been given names. The authorities are now satisfied that you will not be the only people searching for the cone, and that you are likely to have to fight in order to protect the nose cone. Any evidence you can obtain to confirm this view would be very welcome. Of course, a body, dead or alive, would leave no doubt.

The only way from the landing area at Heel is by scaling the cliffs which are 500 ft high. There is a risk, but it can be done. I have some rope aboard but no other climbing gear. You should reckon on it taking you about an hour to climb 300 ft. The cone did not disintegrate on landing. That is all I have to say. Any further questions? No? Then I will leave you to it. Good luck! There is just one other point; I have been ordered to move north west from the area once you have left the ship'.

Some further points which you ascertain during discussions are:

    (a) All timings have been given in GMT.

    (b) Against his training and natural inclinations, the Captain kindly converted all speeds to mph.

    (c) The bad weather which you have been experiencing, was due to spring gales, but the weather is clearing; visibility is good although it will be very cold at night.

    (d) The moon is in the last quarter; sunrise is at 07.00 hrs and sunset at 18.45 hrs.

    (e) The known landing areas are marked on the map and the ship can drop you either two miles off Toe, half a mile off Heel or seven miles off Arch.

    (f) The route along the South coast is good and with luck you could average four mph. Movement elsewhere on the island would be three mph.

    (g) Providing you can make your plan by 10.00 hrs and inform the Captain, he can get to any of the positions off the landing areas by 14.00 hrs and subsequently to another position by 15.30 hrs.

    (h) It is known that the type of small submarine reported carries one small landing boat capable of holding up to six persons.

4 Holistic thinking

The second family of mental aptitudes, the nextdoor neighbours to the analysers, do not have a satisfactory name. In Chapter 2 they were called the *synthesisers,* because synthesis is literally the opposite to analysis. But I cannot forget such phrases as 'synthetic rubber' or 'synthetic dyes', so the word has overtones of the artificial or man-made. Moreover, the logicians – those supreme analysts – have also taken it over to stand for deductive reasoning, or for the dialectic combination of thesis and antithesis into a higher stage of truth (the key idea that Marx borrowed from the philosopher Hegel). But synthesis can be rescued for a wider use. It means essentially the composition or combination of parts or elements to form a whole. The synthesist has a different genre of mind to the analyst.

Another word which points to this rather more mysterious kind of thinking is *holistic.* In 1927 Field Marshal Jan Smuts, a keen agricultural scientist as well as a soldier and a statesman, published a book entitled *Holism and Evolution.* Holism was the word he coined to describe the tendency in nature to produce wholes by ordering or grouping various units together. The essential realities in nature, so Smuts wrote, are these irreducible wholes. They cannot be analysed into their parts without losing this holistic quality. His neologisms – holism and holistic – have now entered our language.

Anybody who has responsibility for the affairs of an organisation – whether the title is chief executive, general manager, president or managing director – has to take a holistic view of it. Indeed in the study of business in its entirety (usually called 'business policy') holistic thinking is the key.

I used the adjective mysterious about holistic thinking quite deliberately, for we cannot analyse holism very far. If we could do that it would cease to be an equal partner in the triumvirate of the mind and become a completed subject to the already over-mighty analysing faculty. But we can coast around it, mapping one or two distinctive features. You should be aware, however, that there is an incipient tension or even civil war in the human mind between analysis and holistic thinking, of which I shall give two examples presently.

The holistic vision

Another word which has done good service as a label for this box of mental attitudes and faculties as *system*. We are surrounded by systems, wholes made up of interacting parts but somehow transcending them.

Look at a candle flame. Why does it maintain approximately the same size and shape throughout its flickering? In this case, the 'parts' are flows of vapourized wax, oxygen and burnt gases – the processes of combustion and diffusion give the interaction between these flows – and these interactions show us at what size and shape the flame will be approximately stable.

The strength of a rope is another example of a holistic property. This strength is a result of interaction among the individual strands, caused by the twisting of the rope. Untwisted, the rope's strength is governed by the weakest strand: twisted, the strands act together and increase their strength.

A holistic mind therefore has a way of looking at things or

people, at the world itself. It is not eager to take things to bits at first glance. Rather it waits until it sees the pattern, the whole, the wood rather than the trees. Equal mental weight is given to the whole in relation to the parts, hence a certain reluctance to dismember. If a nasty schoolboy pulls the legs and wings off a fly he is left with a dead fly: the parts are there but the whole is gone.

Thinkers such as Einstein exemplify this union of formidable powers of analysis with a strain of holistic thinking which seeks out the simple or whole. Weiner Heisenberg, one of the fathers of quantum physics, once spoke to Einstein of the 'almost frightening simplicity and wholeness of the relationships which nature suddenly spreads out before us'. This theme of simplicity, wholeness and beauty – revealed through mathematical formula or detailed experimentation – recurs again and again as nature's mysteries are explored. Whether that simplicity and wholeness is 'really' there or whether it is a projection of holistic human minds, is an important question which we shall touch on later.

Some holistic approaches

The holist then prefers to deal with wholes. In his thinking he tends to dislike overmuch analysis, feeling no compulsive desire to take things or people to bits to see what they are made of. He senses that the whole is always more than the sum of its parts. He sees the wood and not the trees. Latent holists can therefore appear uninterested or even hostile to academic subjects or the academic approach where there is excessive emphasis on analysing.

Indeed the holistic part of our minds is sometimes rather like an Eastern European country under Russian domination. Occasionally the people try to throw off the yoke of analysis, but usually the military moves in and restores order. In the process, however, the holistic reaction is often absorbed into the bloodstream of the subject concerned. Some sort of compromise is eventually struck.

Psychology provides a good example. It became dominated by the scientific analysers around the turn of the century. These people analysed all human experience into its sensory elements. The more holistic thinkers then counterattacked. The Gestalt school of psychology emerged in reaction, basing itself on the following principles:

- an intuitive grasp of the overall significance of behaviour is more desirable than a precise but mechanistic explanation
- we should try to understand relationships between events, not just events themselves
- no event occurs in isolation, but only in a context or field which gives it significance.

In particular, the Gestalt psychologists stressed the tendency of the mind to perceive situations as a whole, rather than as several isolated elements or sensations. For perceptions and reactions are *gestalts,* organised wholes which are more than the sum of their parts, just as a melody is more than its separate notes.

The Gestalt school was labelled anti-analytic. It was not in fact against all analysis, but its members held that the level of analysis should always be appropriate to the nature of reality.

A more contemporary example is the holistic movement in medicine. In 1983 a group of doctors met in London to form the British Holistic Medical Association. The principles it works upon are:

- *mind and body are a unity* and should be treated as such. Human imagination and the power of the unconscious mind, in particular, need to be taken seriously in medicine.
- *nature heals, we help.* Thus holistic medicine looks to ancient and unconscious forces which are vital to our unity with nature.
- *what works with one person may not necessarily work with another.* Medicine should be holistic-related to the person's heredity, personality, environment and lifestyle.·

With orthodox medicine tending to be more materialistic and with specialisation leading to ever greater concentration on symptoms rather than people, these principles behind 'alternative medicine' make good sense, even though the actual expressions of them need careful scrutiny.

52

Thinking holistically about problems

Managers without holistic minds tend to take a narrow view of common problems, interpreting them in single disciplinary or functional ways. 'This is a selling problem', one might say; another, looking at the same phenomenon, calls it 'a production problem'. They are seeing facets of the whole, not the whole itself. Consider this case study:

A small soft drinks company had been pursuing an aggressive expansion policy for several years by continuously adding new flavours to the product range. The managing director was satisfied with the results which showed that the volume of sales had risen quite sharply since the policy had been introduced; the salesforce saw their commissions rising nicely and were pleased too. The only apparent limit to this growth was the difficulty of finding acceptable new flavours. A small laboratory was established to research the problem.

One more immediate cause for concern had developed. The production department was finding it difficult to keep costs down to the anticipated level. In short, productivity was falling as total output went up. The managing director asked the production manager to solve that problem.

Productivity had been defined as 'the volume of output per employee hour' and the production manager found that the hours worked on the shopfloor had risen much faster than total output over the period in question. So, as a first step, he introduced a productivity bonus scheme. This had only a limited effect. After a few months the shop steward began to complain that everyone was working harder for no real benefit.

The next solution to try was reorganising the workflow. Productivity improved, but only marginally. The installation of a new highspeed automatic bottling machine did appear to solve the problem. Soon, however, productivity began to fall again. By now the production manager realised the nub of the problem lay in the fact that each time a new flavour was made, the production line had to be stopped for cleaning. Many flavours were made in very small batches so that down time was actually more than productive time. The greater the number of flavours produced the less time there was for production.

The production manager took a decision: he announced that he was going in for production planning on a four-week cycle. Each

53

flavour would be manufactured only once a month. To do this effectively the sales people had to forecast the demand for each flavour the following month – an exercise they were reluctant to undertake. The managing director intervened to get it underway. The outcome was highly pleasing for everyone until the firm began to run short of cash. Stocks of soft drinks that were being overproduced were building up and left to stand in the stores for weeks rather than days.

Finally, the managing director called a meeting of all senior staff to discuss the situation. During it the accountant suggested that the firm stopped selling the ten least popular flavours. For the total time saved on the shopfloor would, when expressed in money terms, exceed the loss of income. *The business would be better off without them.* The problem was not a production problem, nor a marketing problem, nor a stock-control problem, nor a matter of industrial relations or capital investment; it was a general management problem. To separate it into bits was misguided. Looking at the problem holistically led the managers to adopt the right solution.

Nature and growth

Nature, wholeness, growth are key ideas for the holistic mind. Far from being an artificial or man-made activity, synthesis is the central natural process. Resolution of wholes into their parts – that decaying tree trunk in your garden – are only preludes to a series of syntheses. When we synthesise consciously – putting together elements into a compound – we are only palely imitating what nature is doing all the time. Because we are part of nature however that natural process of growth can happen inside our minds as well as our bodies. *Ideas can start as seeds and then grow.*

This idea of ideas growing is important to the holistic thinker. It may make him reluctant to submit ideas to early analysis by himself or others. A new-born baby is a whole. It grows. But in the first days of its life it needs protection from the chill winds.

Another related distinguishing characteristic of holistic thinkers is that they make considerable use of the *story* method of understanding. They like to know how it began and how it developed.

54

Historians are integrators, as senior managerial leaders have to be. Of the 120 business leaders who answered the questionnaire on p. 30, just over half were graduates. Among these there were as many history graduates as graduates in all kinds of engineering (12 in each); those two subjects come top of the table. 'Why, it is unclear', wrote the researchers, 'but possibly because it is a tough and demanding subject, at which success is a good predictor of a wide range of future achievement'. I would add that a good historian should have a mind balanced between the analytic and holistic poles of thinking: he can do both.

Holistic numeracy

This is the ability to read financial or statistical information holistically. Roy Thomson and Arnold Weinstock certainly possess it. Both read accounting statements like musical conductors read musical scores. Both set up systems by which they received budgets and balance sheets so they could tell how things were going and spot if anything looked wrong.

Lord Weinstock's firm GEC is run as a federation, for it is a huge business with a very wide product range. In Weinstock's view it cannot be managed as a centralised autocracy, especially as he believes in highly professional standards in business decision making – as he puts it, 'all the details, every angle'.

A federated business which delegates to managers the decision making function will only work if financial supervision at the centre is intelligent, continuous and rigorous. Weinstock ensures this by directing every GEC company to supply head office with a regular flow of precise information, including the following basic ratios in their progress reports: sales to capital, sales to stocks, sales to debtors, sales per employee and sales per pound emolument. Weinstock studies these summaries carefully monthly and often writes down the key figures on bits of paper. Any managing director whose figures are not right will get a telephone call. He will be required to say what steps he is going to take to rectify matters. Once a year at a budget session each managing director is cross-examined by Weinstock and his senior colleagues in an extremely blunt way. For Weinstock believes that effective financial controls provide an early warning system for the entire business which ensures that appropriate action is taken as soon as errors are revealed.

Lord Thomson employed a similar method to control his far-flung commercial interests. This holistic way in which he read budgets and financial summaries is instructive:

> These budgets had been set up during the previous two months by the top men of all our various businesses all over the world, who had then gone into head office to argue them with the general manager or managing director of the region or country. All these men in their responsible way had gone over every single cost and determined in the light of their sales experience what their expenditure should be. It was a great spreading complex of items and totals, pluses and minuses, risks and adventures, victories and failures, and yet to one pair of eyes in Toronto, as in London, it all made sense, it all came together in a pattern of activities, diverse and individual, and yet, when I took hold of it like that, a controlled and viable whole.

Note that word 'whole' in the last sentence. This particular ability, which transcends as well as supplements analytical accountancy, probably characterises all really great businessmen.

Holistic thinking then is as relevant to the manager as it is to the artist, doctor or scientist. The capacity to think about organisations and teams, opportunities and problems as wholes is extremely important. As we have seen above, it is possible to think holistically about a budget or a balance sheet if you are gifted that way. Would you say that you are a holistic thinker? You can certainly develop holistic thinking by becoming more aware of its importance and by deliberately refraining from analysis beyond a certain point. Let the whole take shape in your mind's eye.

Signpost

There are several routes that lead from here. The following chapter deals with a specific form of holistic thinking – *concepts*.

After that we shall consider *imagination*, a rather more distant relative of the family.

Chapter 8 looks at *intuition,* which involves holistic thinking done at depth mind level.

Lastly, in Chapter 12, you will notice the theme emerging again in the discussion of creative thinking. Be on the alert for the holistic perspective even where the words 'holistic' and 'synthetic' are not used.

5 Thinking in concepts

This chapter focuses specifically on concepts. As the ability to think conceptually is so important to business leaders it is worth trying to unravel the complexities which surround this aspect of thinking.

The word concept has grown fashionable among managers in recent years. Most managers have it in their vocabularly. But do they know what it means? Concept needs to be distinguished first from the kind of abstract thinking which is implicit in analysing. Let me make it clear at once that all concepts are abstract, some more so and some less. But I want to distinguish concepts as being essentially holistic ideas from the kind of abstract thinking which is implicit in analysing.

What the analyst is trying to do in many cases is to *separate* from the concrete – the specific instances, practices, incidents or particulars – something general. In a word, he is abstracting. What he is left with when he has boiled things down or analysed them is obviously something pretty abstract: certain qualities or attributes of an object view *quite apart,* as it were, from actual material instances.

Now if it is true – and I think it is – that the majority of people do have fairly concrete minds this state of affairs can produce considerable problems of communication. The person who thinks in concrete terms tends to see things in pictures, and to be rooted in the material world of the senses. Concrete minds prefer actual stories, cases, examples or facts. He or she is correspondingly suspicious of anything general or abstract. Hence the very word *abstract* in our language carries such unpleasant overtones as:

- difficult to understand
- remote from apprehension
- insufficiently factual
- theoretical
- impersonal
- detached
- visionary

You can see why concrete thinkers find any contact with those who view life in abstract terms rather unsatisfactory!

Perhaps the most serious divide in Western society, the 'two cultures', is not between science and arts, rich and poor, or managers and workforce, but between *concrete* and *abstract* thinkers. Most managers prefer to keep their feet on the ground and let others float upwards into the clouds of abstraction, travelling in baskets of logic strung beneath balloons full of hot air. Occasionally the balloonists drop the odd bombshell, but mostly it seems they can safely be ignored.

Here is an extract from an article by W.F. Younger, Managing Director of Hay-MSL Management Consultants which illustrates the point well:

> As a consultant and a former industrial manager, I have had the privilege of working on industrial problems sometimes with teams of shop floor people and sometimes with groups of managers. One of the facts of life I have observed over the years is that managers and work people are increasingly bringing different vocabularies to the same situation. The new managers

have been trained to think analytically and in abstract, to use words which are designed to convince on the basis of reasoning and intellect. They have been educated to the ideal of 'the rational manager', seeking solutions which are based on careful study and reflection, on analysis and evaluation of facts. They have been taught to communicate on a factual analytic basis.

People with less formal academic education, however, tend to have a smaller vocabulary. They also use a different vocabulary, based on the dominance of physical activity in their life. They deal with practical, visible, tangible things not symbols or abstract thought, and they expect their leaders to be visible, to be practical and to be available. Many of the shop floor words are vividly descriptive with emotional overtones rather than with cold analytical meanings. I remember a production operator saying to me, 'By the time you take the four-letter words out of my job description there'll be — all left'. His description was right. He had a filthy job carried out in appalling conditions.

Manual workers distrust arguments based on abstract analysis; they feel that they will be outsmarted by those who have learned more of the words and more of the rules of that game. Unhappy past experience of the consequences of cold economic reasoning, often leads them to be more responsive to those calls which are to the emotions of the spirit and the heart than to the ascetic calculations of the brain.

In the exercise of rating key attributes in order of value for their work, you may recall that the successful chief executives taking part rated 'analytical ability' in seventh place, and 'capacity for abstract thought' collected the wooden spoon: it was put in bottom place out of the 25 attributes listed. The chief executives were probably unclear that analytical ability *implies* capacity for abstract thought. For the objects of analysis, to repeat the point, are relations, laws or generalisations. The analyst is trying to separate from the concrete (specific instances, practices or incidents) something general. He is after an essence. In a word, he is abstracting.

Concepts

Had the compilers of that questionnaire used the phrase 'ability to think conceptually' the latter may have been given a higher rating by the chief executives. A concept looks like the abstraction arrived at by analysis, but it has a different feel. The distinguishing features are, first, that it is a whole (more than the sum of its parts), and secondly that it has a life story of its own: it is a living, growing entity. Concepts are our intellectual equivalents to the systems or organisms we see all around us: trees, birds, gardens and so on. They are living wholes.

Consider the following story:

Henry Saunders is a senior manager in Tarmac International, with experience mainly on the personnel and work study side. He is anxious to broaden his experience and has applied for a marketing area manager's job, reporting directly to the marketing director. The evening before the final interview he meets on the train going home one of the directors who will be on his selection panel next day. 'Of course I cannot tell you what we shall want to know in detail, Henry,' he confided, 'but we shall certainly ask you about your concept of marketing. I am very keen on team building too, you know. Well, there it is, I get off here – Good luck!'

If you were Henry Saunders, preparing for that interview tomorrow, how would you define the concept of marketing? Is it, for example, the same as selling? What is your concept of a team? Would you not agree that in a true team the whole is more than the sum of the parts?

You cannot define or analyse a concept completely to everyone's satisfaction. Trying to define concepts in the narrow sense is like putting wild animals into cages. But you can make real progress in understanding them.

In this work of explaining concepts habitual resort to the dictionary can help. But beware of what philosophers call the Word-Concept Fallacy. This is the notion that any word corresponds to a concept. Usually they do not. Names of concepts are more like labels rather than definitions – they tell you what box to open. Definitions give the ways in which we can reasonably use words, but a concept is always more than the sum of definitions. No one has ever defined the concept of leadership, for example; it is too rich for that. But they have said how they intend to use the word. Fair enough.

Society could not exist unless there was at least rough agreement on how words can legitimately be used. You can of course define a term in any way you choose. You can call a spade a pickaxe if you like. But you must expect to be widely misunderstood.

When the analyst is confronted with an unfamiliar concept he flies to the nearet dictionary and analyses it (or follows the lexicographer's attempts to do) into its constituent meanings. He may then be under the false impression that he understands the concept. But dictionaries tend to give you synonyms or antonyms, words of roughly the same or opposite meaning. Your dictionary may define 'friend' as a companion, associate or colleague. But these do not fully analyse the concept of friendship: they are like three more darts thrown at the dartboard of friendship. If you get the pattern of darts right the concept may begin to take shape in your mind.

A holistic thinker setting about understanding a concept would want some analysis, coupled with some knowledge of the history of the concept. Even concepts like friendship have a history. That harks back to my earlier point, that concepts are holistic: they are flowers or fruits grown from small seeds in history. Indeed *concept* and *conception* – the act of becoming pregnant – are from the same Latin root. The sexual analogy is apt. A concept is something conceived in the mind. It may begin, as in the case of creative thinking, with some seed thought becoming planted in the mind which then forms itself naturally over time. This process may be aided by reading and reflecting on experience. Obviously concepts grow in our minds – providing the soil and climate are favourable – so that understanding of them develops. Other people's books and management courses are merely fertilizers.

Something to think about

Here is a standard textbook definition of the concept of management:

A manager is responsible for more work than he can do himself, so that the factor which distinguishes him is that people work for him; he is set over subordinates to whom he delegates specific parts of the task for which he is responsible. This is not to say that the manager will not himself be responsible as a subordinate to some higher authority, nor that those under him may not in their own right be managers.

Now consult in a library two or three good dictionaries and reconstruct the evolution of the concept of management in order to supplement this definition.

The following are examples of concepts related to management, worth exploring in a similar way: alienation, strategy, communication, finance, motivation, money, opportunities, strengths and weaknesses, wealth, participation, equal pay for equal work, personality, the right to work, organisation, power, culture, self, monetarism, redundancy, social responsibility, intelligence, profit, profitability, productivity and efficiency.

Conceptual thinking and decision making

You see that the above list is long and, of course, far from complete. Therefore in an organisation not all managers will be thinking about all concepts in the same depth. The range and depth of concepts in the minds of marketing and finance manager will probably differ. But there is one basic concept all the senior managers should discuss and agree about: the concept of their own organisation. What business it is in, what are its strengths and weaknesses, and what are its purposes and aims?

The evidence suggests that company boards rarely make time for such conceptual thinking. Trees die from the top downwards, and management's failure to think until it hurts usually starts in the boardroom.

Actually it is doubtful if the monthly meeting of the board, which lasts two or three hours and has an invariably pressing agenda of short-term items, is really the place for conceptual thinking. Better to go away to an hotel for a day or two.

For it is important to compartmentalise conceptual thinking from decision making. They are obviously related, for our concepts or 'constructs' of reality will largely determine what we do and how we do it. If my concept of friendship is basically that it is a temporary league of two self-interested people using one another to their selfish advantage, you will not be surprised if I drop you like a hot brick when I have no further use for you. But decision making is not the time for conceptual discussion, at least not at any depth. We all have to think and decide on the basis of concepts anyway which are indefinable and inexhaustible, so our knowledge of them is incomplete.

The case of the summit meeting

The following example shows how wires can get crossed between conceptual thinking and decision making. Consider the lessons it has for the organisation you know best.

On 22 May 1980 Michael Edwardes, Chairman of British Leyland and two of his directors attended a working dinner with the Prime Minister, Mrs Margaret Thatcher, at No. 10 Downing Street. They had come to discuss the future of the company now that the rise in the pound's value had eroded the increased competitiveness British Leyland had achieved through cutting costs and increasing productivity.

'The Prime Minister was very much in the chair', wrote Edwardes later.[1] Her team included the Chancellor of the Exchequer and the Minister for Industry. 'She was in an enquiring mood, somewhat reminiscent of the Spanish Inquisition. "Now what's all this about? You're not going to ask for more money?", was her opening salvo. When I replied that we would certainly need some hundreds of millions of additional funds, this immediately established a frosty atmosphere for the early part of the evening'.

There followed a discussion of BL's problems and possible solutions, such as privatisation of sections. 'What could BL do about it? – that was more to the point', said the Prime Minister. Edwardes outlined some short-term steps. 'Throughout the evening it was impossible to tell from her expression whether or not we were making headway in building our case for the future'. They ended by discussing large wage settlements in the public sector, interest levels and the value of the pound.

'By the end of the evening we all agreed that no proposals were left on the table, because the BL Board were not ready to put forward positive recommendations – therefore no decisions were sought. We had had a useful exchange of views, and the climate which at the beginning of the evening had been frosty to cool, warmed up just a little. We trooped out into Downing Street at ten minutes past eleven.

'I pause here to reflect on whether we were right to have initiated this type of debate. In mid-year, between plans, one can only talk in very broad terms. We were postulating concepts – concepts which could not be quantified in any precise way for some months – and foreshadowed problems for 1981 which would only become crystallised when we submitted the 1981 Plan towards the end of 1980. We had reason to believe from subsequent feedback that the Prime Minister found this unsatisfactory. Our lack of precision, our lack of quantification of likely sums involved, was seen by her as a weakness – whereas we saw the working dinner as an opportunity to flag up problems on the horizon. As a Board we were used to dealing with concepts at the profile stage, and specific at the plan or budget stage. We thought we were being helpful in doing this, but she expected a debate of the latter type, and our 'broad' approach was read as a lack of professionalism . . . she had no desire to repeat the exercise; it was the first and last working dinner!'

Reflective thinking

The pressures on managers at the more senior levels, as described in Chapter 1, militate against high quality conceptual thinking in organisations, but you as an individual leader should be trying to change that state of affairs as you near the top. Frederick R. Kappel, former chief executive of the American Telephone and Telegraph Company, emphasises that need in the following passage. He distinguishes between reflective thinking and action thinking:

> I use the term 'reflective' thinking to cover the mental activity required to ask searching (and sometimes embarrassing) questions about the adequacy of the current operation. This kind of thinking can be disturbing to some men at the center of successful action, because they may see it as dealing with remote abstractions, with theories of management that seem impractical, and with visionary speculations about the future. The success of a business today, largely based on action thinking, gives the opportunity to build vitality but it doesn't do the building. For that, reflective thinking is essential.

> Looking at the business of the Bell System, I know we can reach out immediate goals without a great deal of reflective thinking. But I doubt that we can build vitality for tomorrow without a lot of it, for this is the way we get deeper understanding of our problems. I make this point because I believe the pressures to meet the problems of the say tend to discourage reflective thinking, and when this happens to a business it will surely lose vitality.[2]

You can see that the enemy of what Kappel calls reflective thinking is that distaste for abstract thinking. Managers see themselves as practical doers, as action-oriented, and not as abstract thinkers.

Concepts, however, are not necessarily abstract. There is nothing abstract about the concept of the hatchback car. But concepts do get you away from the particular. There is undeniably an abstract or general aspect to them, which can make them *look* the same as the results of abstractive or analytical thinking. But concepts are not merely generalisations. They include ideas of what *ought* to be the case as well as what *is* in fact the case. The concept of friendship cannot be inductively reached by studying 300 pairs of friends, because it includes ideas of what friendship *ought* to be – and you cannot get a value from a fact. The concept of an electrically powered family car, for example, will include much imaginative thinking about what *might* be.

Values, ideals, possibilities – even more abstract? Not really. The dichotomy between concrete and abstract is false if pressed too far anyway, for generalisations must refer to particulars. The analyst is in fact ranging up and down the scales of general/particular, whole/part. So can the conceptual thinker. As you may have found, an (abstract) concept like management reveals a core of concrete reference: *manus,* the Latin for hand, handling a horse, handling a ship at sea, handling an army, and so on. It comes from the same root as manipulate, which makes one think even more.

These internal concrete images can always be supplemented by analogy. Motivation for example has a subsidiary concept which is extremely real, at least for donkey owners: 'the carrot and the stick'.

66

Abstract thinkers have always had a certain intellectual snobbery about their more practically minded counterparts. When Plato visited Syracuse in 387 BC he soundly denounced Eudoxus and Archytas for debasing the excellence of geometry by making her descend from the world of ideas to the world of the senses and to make use of material objects which are more appropriate to tradespeople. The practical interests of these two thinkers foreshadowed the work of the great mathematician and engineer Archimedes, who designed the fortifications of Syracuse more than a hundred years later. Archytas, the founder of the study of mechanics, and Eudoxus the creator of the general theory of proposition in geometry, had solved together the problem of doubling the cube by using two cylinders. As Plutarch comments:

> Thus through mechanics they gave geometry an additional variety and elegance; and they also succeeded in solving by mechanical methods certain problems which could not be solved purely theoretically. That problem for example of two mean proportional lines, which cannot be solved geometrically without the aid of instruments called mesolabes taken from conic sections.

Down the centuries, more concrete minded and practical or applied thinkers have returned shot for shot, and despised the abstract, theoretical or general thinkers as the intellectual drones of society. Of course it is a pointless war. Science, and especially technology, reveal the need for both poles of thought. Concepts have a strategic importance in this war because they *can* occupy the middle ground. They do engage the holistic mind which is much more common than the analytical one. Concepts do blend the particular and the general concrete and abstract in a satisfying way. They do introduce value and imagination. As such, if well communicated, most concepts are well within reach of the workforce, especially as improved education and training equips and extends our range for conceptual thinking.

Conclusions

'No great improvements in the lot of mankind are possible, until a great change takes place in the fundamental constitution of their modes of thought', wrote John Stuart Mill. The quality of your concepts and your ability to develop them, as an individual, as an organisation, is the foundation of good decision making. Aim to have clear concepts. Define them as well as you can. Be open to new light on them from unexpected sources.

References

1   Edwardes, M., *Back from the Brink*, Collins and Pan Books, 1984.
2   Kappel, Frederick R., *Vitality in a Business Enterprise*, McGraw-Hill, New York, 1960.

6 Imaginative thinking

Successful chief executives rate *imagination* high in the list of attributes which they value most. But what is imagination and how does it contribute to business success? This chapter seeks to answer those questions and to enable you to develop your own imaginative powers.

'As a rule', wrote Kenneth Grahame, author of *The Wind in the Willows*, 'grown-up people are fairly correct on matters of fact; it is the higher gift of imagination that they are so sadly to seek'.

Imagination almost certainly belongs to the family of synthesisers. Neither the analyst nor the critic are necessarily imaginative, but the synthesist is likely to be.

There is definitely a family relationship between imagination and holistic thinking. Take as an example this description of the crucial phase in composition by one of the world's great composers, Wolfgang Amadeus Mozart:

> First bits and crumbs of the piece come and gradually join together in my mind; then the soul getting warmed to the work, the thing *grows* more and more, and I spread it out broader and clearer, and at last it gets almost finished in my head, even when it is a long piece, so that I can *see* the *whole* of it at a single glance in my mind, as if it were a beautiful painting or a handsome human being; in which way I do not hear it in my *imagination* at all as a succession – the way it must come later – but all at once as it were. It is a rare feast. All the *inventing and making* goes on in me is in a beautiful strong dream. But the best of all is the hearing of it all at once.

I have put key words or phrases in italics to emphasise the proximity of the two concepts of holistic and imaginative work in this particular passage.

Some imaginative thinkers, such as Nobel Prize winner Sir Lawrence Bragg, who pioneered X-ray crystallography, have the capacity to imagine things in three dimensions in their minds. Nikola Tesla, an extremely productive technological innovator (fluorescent lights, the AC generator, the 'Tesla' coil), apparently had extraordinary powers of visualisation. According to his biographer Tesla 'could project before his eyes a picture complete in every detail, of every part of the machine. These pictures were more vivid than any blueprint'. Further, Tesla claimed to be able to test his devices mentally, by having them run for weeks – after which time he would examine them thoroughly for signs of wear.[1]

Thinking in pictures

Our minds have a fundamental visual capacity: we not only see things but we can shut our eyes and remember the picture of what we have seen.

That is one pole of the imagination. In the piece quoted above Mozart said 'I can see the whole of it at a single glance in my mind, as if it were a beautiful painting or a handsome human being'. What he saw was something that had not existed before. Imagination for him was the spearhead of inventing and making. That gives us the other pole of the imagination. But there are other shades of these abilities as well.

Table 6.1 shows the remarkable range of imaginative abilities, from memory function at one end of the scale to creative imagination at the other. Fantasy is central to such practices as brainstorming, often taught on management courses.

Having answered the questions in Figure 6.1, reflect on whether you imagine in colour and in three-dimensions. Does your imagination have real thrust and life – can it get you off the runways of perceived reality?

Table 6.1

FACTS	ABILITIES
Recalling	The ability to bring back an idea to mind something not actually present to the senses, such as your house or car
Visualising	The ability to form a picture of something not experienced in its entirety, such as what it would be like for you to walk on the moon
Creating	The ability to form an image or whole of something actually non-existent at present, such as a new product
Foreseeing	The ability to see a development or outcome before it materialises
Fantasy	The ability to invent the novel and unreal by altering or combining the elements of reality in a particularly unrestrained and extravagant way

How imaginative are you?

Put YES or NO
in each box

Can you recall visually with great accuracy?
Imagine your last holiday and see how much
detail you can see in the mental pictures. ☐

Would you describe yourself as good at
visualising things which you have not
experienced directly yourself? Could you, for
example, imagine accurately what it would
be like to be a member of the opposite sex?
Or prime minister? Or your own secretary? ☐

Has anyone commended you for your
imagination within the last year? ☐

Have you invented or made anything recently,
at work or in leisure time, which definitely
required imagination? ☐

Do you tend to foresee accurately what
happens before the event? ☐

Do you fantasise about your work or career? ☐

Do you paint or draw? ☐

Do you find it easy to choose colour schemes
when you have to redecorate your room? ☐

Do you find that you can think up names for
such things as babies, pets, houses? ☐

Have you ever written a story or poem? ☐

Figure 6.1

Practice in using your imagination

1 Imagine you are climbing Everest by yourself and without oxygen. You are a thousand metres from the summit.
   (a) Sit down and make a meal for yourself. Work through each of your five senses to complete the scene in your mind.
   (b) You are now pressing on to the summit. What can you see? What are you touching? What are your feelings? What colours can you see?
   (c) Now you are on the summit. You have a camera with you. Set it up on a rock. Stand back. Now compose in detail the photograph you have taken. Turn it into a three-dimensional picture.
2 A new creature has been discovered in the jungles of South America which is destined to replace the dog and cat as our most popular domestic pet. Briefly describe it in 200 words and draw a picture of it. Give it a name.
3 Morwenstow is a small village on the north Cornwall coast. One Sunday evening during the Napoleonic Wars the vicar was preaching at evensong in the village church. A great storm raged outside. Suddenly the congregation heard a great crash. A vessel had struck the rocks. Everyone rushed out of the church and with the vicar at their head they hurried down the steep path to the bay. In the dusk they saw the smashed wreck of a three-masted schooner, its debris scattered on the beach. There was apparently only one survivor lying unconscious on the sand. He was a swarthy man, dressed in a sea captain's uniform. But when they turned him over a look of terror came over the vicar's face. . . .

Now continue the story.

You may find it fanciful to be asked to compose a short story. But there is a relation between an author's and a businessman's imagination: both are growing something from small seeds. Therefore do not be put off attempting the above exercise because it seems to have nothing to do with management.

Thinking and imagination

It is helpful to stress the pictorial dimension in imagination but, beyond a certain point, it is better to use the word in a much

"Fill her up!"

broader sense. Tolstoy's *War and Peace,* which has no pictures, is a much greater work than comics which are full of them. Avoid becoming hooked on trying to see or make mental pictures: you can think imaginatively without them. Equally you can imagine without thinking.

Let me illustrate. A mother, anxious when her child has not come home from school, imagines all sorts of scenes. She is the passive prey of horrible fantasies, which come into her mind successively in a way she cannot control. Emotion and imagination have joined forces. Her imagaination is hyperactive and her powers of thinking unexercised. She is panic-stricken. In this situation thought and imagination are diametrical opposites.

In other situations we are inclined to distinguish them as just different. For example, if you read a scientific account of the geography of northern Greenland you might be thinking analytically about the climate, flora and fauna, while also trying to visualise what the country looks like and how you would live there. You will be thinking like a physical geographer while also composing a scenario for yourself in your imagination.

But there is a third group of situations in which a person's thinking and imagination are really inseparable – his thinking is *imaginative thinking*. Take the good detective or a top-class manager. In trying to work out problems they need to be both fertile in imagining feasible hypotheses and also careful about their data and what can be properly deduced. They must think imaginatively, but also in a coherent, methodical and unfanciful way.

Why, then, has not imagination been given its proper place in management training and education? First, we are still inclined to treat arithmetical computation – the sort of thing computers do – as the most characteristic exercise of the highly trained mind. I do not know where this assumption comes from. Computation, though very important, is a comparatively low form of thinking, increasingly delegated now to machines. Adding and subtracting, multiplying and dividing, hardly give much scope for originality, flair, talent, horse sense, intuition, judgement or constructiveness.

Second, we find it hard to rid ourselves of the assumption that imagination is exercised only in dreaming up fictional things or happenings. William Shakespeare declared that 'imagination bodies forth the forms of things unknown'. He did invent a living world of fictional characters and incidents. But Leonardo da Vinci and Thomas Edison had good imaginations too. Prospero and Hamlet are imaginary people, but the submarine and helicopter, the electric light bulb and telephone are not imaginary objects, though it needed a combination of imagination and technical knowledge to invent them.

More practice in using your imagination

Einstein imagined how the world would look if you travelled on the back of a sunbeam. The question had first occurred to him as a child and in adulthood he acquired the intellectual equipment and knowledge to answer it. List three imaginative questions of this kind – involving fantasy – which could revolutionise familiar concepts in your working environment.

Imaginative thinking in action

Imaginative thinking is not limited, however, to inventing things. The detective or the manager are customarily not inventing or making anything but they are still thinking imaginatively. They are also linked in that they both have an adversary – the criminal in one case and competitors in another. Sportsmen and soldiers share that factor as well.

Let me illustrate again. When a famous football player is being praised for playing imaginatively, he is not being praised for fantasising in his armchair or writing novels about football. Rather he is seen to do things like the following:

- in trying to get past the opposing player he does not use the same jink or swerve time after time – or he may do so three times just in order to surprise him on the fourth occasion with a different change of direction
- he does not assume that his team-mate will pass out to the right, as he did the last five times – he is ready for it to come to him this time
- he realises swiftly that there is a gap likely to open up where, at the moment, no gap can be seen

In other words, he is quick to anticipate, to see and act upon things which are out of the ordinary. He surprises his opponents and yet is not taken by surprise. He exploits the unexpected and the lack of routine.

This imaginative thinking on the football field has nothing to do with whether or not the player concerned writes fictional stories about football. It also has nothing to do with the rational and logical thinking prized so highly by the academics. Ron Greenwood, as manager of the England football team, said that 'football is a battle of wits' for which a combination of physical and mental attributes is needed:

A football brain is quite different from an academic brain. I coached at Oxford University for seven years and if the students had had the right kinds of football brains they would have been the best team in the world. But they didn't and they weren't. A man who can hardly read or write can have a great football brain.

Imagination of a kind also helps the criminal. The following parable illustrates that imagination, together with the entrepreneurial spirit, can flourish, in the most limiting circumstances. Consider this story:

Bernard Leach had a worldwide reputation as a potter, and his pots were selling for hundreds, and in some cases thousands of pounds, with public auction rooms keen to cash in on the wave of popularity. Two prisoners in Featherstone Prison near Wakefield in Britain were quick to realise the implications of this fact for them. They were attending pottery classes early in 1981 and set about copying Leach's work from photographs in books and magazines. They impressed the prison authorities on one occasion by their enthusiasm for the craft by making 14 'Leach' pots. Even more significantly a Bernard Leach 'seal' BL was stamped onto the base of the wares.

Prisoners are not allowed to sell the pots they make but can pay a nominal sum of a few pence per item and give them to friends and family. These potters handed their pots to a friend who was an antique dealer, who duly placed them for sale at London auction houses, including Christies, where they sold for prices between £200 and over £1000. Their only mistake was to put too many onto the market too quickly. After their detection one of the three prisoners explained that he had put BL on the pots because one of his aliases was Bernard Lee!

Imaginative thinking of this kind is clearly relevant to fields other than criminal forgery in prison, detective work or football. War, for example, calls for it constantly. The fighter pilot in the Battle of Britain had to use his imagination as he ducked and weaved his way through interminable dogfights. Successful generals down the ages have shown the same capacity. Winston Churchill once wrote 'nearly all the battles which are regarded as the masterpieces of the military art, have been battles of manoeuvre in which very often the enemy has found himself defeated by some novel device, some unexpected thrust or strategy. In such battles the losses of the victor have been small and the enemy is left puzzled as well as beaten'.

In business your next move is not blueprinted for you. It is true that you do not have total freedom. You do not have the freedom of action of someone writing a television script or the composer of a poem. But you are like a person crossing an unmapped plateau. You have to think up for yourself and then suspiciously try out possible ways of getting where you want to be – and the solutions to these problems are not in books nor can they be recalled from your memory bank. For you have never been here before. You have to originate or innovate, and you cannot innovate by following established precedents or by applying common recipes. John Sainsbury, chairman of the highly successful chain of grocery supermarkets which bears his name, states:

> The characteristic in a good manager which I appreciate almost above all else is that of imagination. The good manager has to be imaginative in order to be a successful innovator. Success in that respect brings not only a valuable contribution to any enterprise, but also the considerable personal satisfaction of creative achievement.
>
> It is imagination which is needed to anticipate events and to respond to change. It is only those with a lively imagination who can really develop sensitive understanding of others, be they customers, colleagues or shop floor workers. To be able to do that is a vital ingredient of success in commerce or industry.

Yes, but can you develop imaginative thinking?

We all have a capacity to synthesise. In widely differing degrees we are all inventive. For example, we make casual little jokes of our own. They may not be very witty or bring the house down, but they are *new* jokes and not the 'Did you hear the one about . . .' variety. Notice, now, that if we are asked to say how we came to think of a joke we are stumped for an answer. There seems to be no technique or recap or method of joke making. So we reply vaguely, 'Oh! It just came to me'.

Yet inventive thinking, while not a matter of mere technique is not a matter of mere luck either. You can be sure that the professional comedian does research on jokes. He may keep a card index of them and of the audience reactions. Perhaps people in one country laugh at mother-in-law jokes more than audiences in other lands. He may have classified jokes into such basic types. He may even have tried to analyse and generalise about the concept of humour. What is it that makes people laugh? What situations are intrinsically funny? He may note relationships. For example, humour is connected to our sense of proportion, which is why we laugh at a very large person riding a very small bicycle, or at some preposterous boast or claims by the comedian. Humour, like creative thinking, often happens when two lines of apparently unconnected thought suddenly intersect. You may have heard about the farmer who liked chicken legs so much, he bred a four-legged chicken. Unfortunately, he could not catch it.

Have you come across any imaginative thinking at work recently? The same principles certainly apply in the sphere of management. You may like to do some research on examples of imaginative thinking in business and to reflect upon the situations in which it is called for. These activities will not in themselves make you more imaginative but they will stimulate your interest and enrich your concept of the imaginative and resourceful manager.

Sportsmen find it helpful to imagine themselves in future situations: relaxed, confident and masterful. Imagine yourself at the next committee meeting saying, 'Look, are we not falling into our customary rut again. Can't we be more imaginative?' Imagine the look of amazement which will come over the faces of your colleagues!

You work for the pharmaceutical division of a multinational. You have just invented a simple cure for the common cold and the whole world will be grateful. You will become rich and famous when your discovery is confirmed, as it surely will be. Imagine the scene in the New York boardroom of your company at a reception held in your honour. See the riches you are about to acquire. If you think that such fantasising is 'unreal' it is worth recalling that Leonardo da Vinci indulged in it while working mentally on his designs for a submarine and a machine for mass-producing needles.

Changing your self-image, the way you see yourself, is probably the most potent way of unlocking the doors of the practical imagination. If you do not apply imagination to yourself you are unlikely to apply it in life.

More practice in using your imagination

- Do you see yourself as a rational manager who is sometimes imaginative, or as an imaginative manager who is also analytical?
- When you visualise yourself – the concept of you – do you see considerable potential waiting to be realised?
- Imagine yourself in five years time as a chief executive with a proven reputation for imaginative action. How did you acquire that reputation? Create three more-or-less credible fantasies to explain your sudden emergence from the pack – apart from marrying the chairman's ill-favoured daughter.

Imagination in perspective

Imagination should not be promoted to top place in the hierarchy of thinking abilities. It should be a team player, not the captain. It is the vanguard, the advance scouting party, of thinking. The specific role of imagination is to lead us into innovating, inventing, creating, exploring, risk-taking, and adventuring.

The manager who knowingly ventures off or beyond the beaten track, the path of well-trodden expectations, is showing some degree of imagination. His business ventures may turn out to be fruitless, random or crazy. For managers who dream, dreams may be pathfinders, but they may also lead to the bankruptcy courts. Of those who depart from well-established ways only a few are explorers. 'Imaginative', 'inventive' and 'adventurous' are terms of praise, but equally 'fanciful', 'reckless' and 'crazy' describe those who are failed imaginative thinkers.

We should therefore be on guard against any tendency to glorify the notion of imagination as an end itself. People sometimes forget that a lively imagination can also be a silly one. Scope for originality is also freedom to be a crackpot. Both the genius and the crank are imaginative thinkers – some are both at the same time.

Yet imagination covers some crucial qualities in the business leader. There will be plenty of situations in your future career calling upon your powers of originating, inventing, improvising, discovering, innovating, exploring, experimenting, and of knowingly leaving the beaten track. Can you imagine yourself now doing all those things?

Reference

1 O'Neill, J.J., *Prodigal Genius: The Life of Nikola Tesla*, Panther, 1981.

7 Valuing

Valuing is one of the three essential components in thinking. We cannot avoid it. This chapter asks you to reflect on the concept of value and, in particular, on the importance of the value of truth in decision making.

After *ability to take decisions* and *leadership*, the executive heads of British industry put in third place *integrity* in the list of 25 attributes. Lord Slim defined integrity by its effects: 'it is the quality which makes people trust you'. But what is it about integrity that induces that feeling?

The word itself means wholeness. It is a holistic word. One is tempted to conclude that integrity as such does not exist; perhaps it is the pattern of all your qualities. But there are some distinctive elements. Integrity implies adherence to a code of moral, artistic or other values. It suggests, too, trustworthiness and incorruptibility to a degree that one is incapable of being false to a trust, responsibility or pledge.

At the core of integrity lies the value of truth. Its most

common synonym is *honesty,* the refusal to lie, steal or deceive in any way. These qualities of character rest upon the assumption that you can *perceive* the truth in a situation. That ability is obviously vital to good decision making. For decision making rests upon two pillars:

- establishing the truth
- knowing what to do

Because managers are prey to time pressures, and tend to be action oriented anyway, they are inclined to skimp on the first and move too quickly on to the more congenial second.

The autonomy of valuing

To repeat an earlier point, valuing is a distinctive function. Most of us are now aware that you cannot get a value from a fact. No amount of reasoning, logical argument, emotional appeal or factual information can *prove* a value. Nor, as a famous phrase has it, can you get an *ought* from an *is*.

Moreover like imagining, valuing appears sometimes to be quite separate from the reasoning processes we call thinking. The professor of botany, who spends his life analysing and comparing the 250 or so varieties of buttercup in the world, might suddenly spot a host of yellow buttercups blazing in an Alpine meadow and say 'How beautiful they look!'

There are times, however, when valuing and thinking are virtually inseparable. By chance, the day before writing this chapter, I took an old telescope into Christies in London, intending to sell it. The expert at the reception desk turned it over, examined it, tapped it. 'No maker's name', he mused, as if to himself, 'but still that need not matter'. Looking up he said, 'This brass section here would probably have been covered by leather'. More musing. 'It's worth about £30. I am afraid we cannot sell it here, because the cost of doing so would exceed our commission. Try a local saleroom'.

You can see there clearly two parts or pillars of decision making. First, the truth about the telescope and its value had to be established. That if you like was the first objective. Truth in this sense is an account of things as they are. The most immediate and most widely used synonym is real or reality. Reality is complex and has different levels; truth is the grasp, always partial, always subjectively conditioned, that we have of reality.

The second phase was a decision based upon that appraisal. The Christies expert had three options open to him:

- yes, we should like to put your telescope in our next sale of optical instruments.
- no, we suggest you sell it elsewhere.
- wait, may I do more research on it and consult my colleagues? We will let you know our decision.

In this case his information about the telescope – the truth as he perceived it – led him unerringly to the second option. The prior work of establishing the truth, in other words, made the work of decision effortless. In management those two distinct but related activities – thinking it out and deciding what to do – need to be held apart by a deliberate act of mind.

Thinking must precede and guide action to be effective. Yet there seems to be a lack of awareness by many executives that the effectiveness of any action – excluding luck – rests on the quality of the thinking which precedes it. From your experience do you agree?

A policy for thinkers

Valuing is, of course, partly subjective anyway: it involves a valuing faculty which we all have. But is it wholly subjective or is it partly objective? Do I really see the truth about that telescope or am I reading it into the thing? After all, I am told that the red pen with which I am writing is not red at all – things do not have colour – it is just reflecting light in a certain way that activates my 'red' eyecells.

We obviously cannot prove the case either way, but we can get near to it. Take, for example, the mass exterminations perpetrated in concentration camps such as Belsen and Dachau during World War Two. Even Bertrand Russell, who held the view that truth was subjective, had to admit that evil was there, whatever the opinions of philosophers. The evil did not exist in the minds of some beholders; it was an objective quality or value intrinsic to the place and the people who staffed its mass-production methods of death.

Whatever your philosophical or religious views, provided you have not come down irrevocably on the 'truth does not exist' side, I should like to persuade you to adopt a central policy as a thinker (which you probably do already, consciously or unconsciously). And that is to *assume* that truth exists. For that act of faith produces the best results. (The proposition that 'there are no bad followers, only bad leaders' may not be true, but it is still an excellent maxim to remember.)

The policy of behaving as if truth was an object, that we *discover* truth rather than invent it, has been enormously helpful in science. There is a link here with religion. Albert Einstein, who stood in the Jewish tradition, reflected that fundamental belief in the 'givenness' of truth and other values springing from the mind of some holistic 'other'. He believed that God might pose difficult problems but would never break the rules posing unanswerable ones. Blind chance was never the answer: 'God does not play dice with the world'. He once described his fundamental quest for truth by saying 'I want to know how God created the world. I am not interested in this or that phenomenon, in the spectrum of this or that element. I want to know his thoughts, the rest are details'.

Einstein is an especially apt example. His theory of relativity has had a profound influence. When such fundamental concepts as absolute space and absolute time were proved to be relative – one man's *now* is another man's *then*, for *now* is a subjective conception valid only for an observer with one specific frame of reference – it was widely believed that all values or concepts, such as truth, were equally relative. One man's truth is another man's lie – it all depends on where you stand.

This popular impression rests largely on a misunderstanding of what Einstein actually discovered. When the Archbishop of Canterbury asked Einstein to comment on the common view that his theory had altered human values, the physicist replied: 'Do not believe a word of it. It makes no difference. It is purely abstract science'. Elsewhere he wrote:

The meaning of relativity has been widely misunderstood. Philosophers play with the word, like a child with a doll. Relativity, as I see it, merely denotes that certain physical and mechanical facts which have been regarded as positive and permanent, are relative to certain other facts in the sphere of physics and mechanics.

Scientists do not have to hold any kind of religious belief in a deity, however intangible and impersonal, to adopt the policy of believing that truth is 'out there', that it is like a quarry in a dense forest to be trapped, hunted or cornered. The community of scientists do act precisely as if that is what it believes, and the results have indeed been spectacular.

In management I suggest the same policy has more to be said for it than any other. If you act on the assumption that there is a truth 'out there' you will struggle to find it, knowing that only decisions based on truth are likely to be successful. We certainly know the converse to be true: if a decision is based on faulty evidence it is unlikely to be successful.

Ask yourself the following questions:

Can you identify a situation at work where you would be compelled to resign on grounds of conscience?

Have you ever, in your career, refused to tell a lie and borne the consequences?

Do you act as if you believe that truth is 'out there' when you are thinking?

'Truth is great and shall prevail, when none care whether it prevail or not'. Do you think that the truth has a power or life of its own: that it will assert itself if only we allow it to do so?

To summarise: valuing and values can be seen as a quite distinct and autonomous family. The capacity to value is universal. The actual values we adopt or express in action will be conditioned by society, but it does not necessarily follow that values as such do not have objective reality. That may or may not be so, depending upon the ultimate nature of the universe. But the practical belief that value is there has paid off in science. It makes you alert to look for something and not to be satisfied until you have found it. You may be sceptical but you are not cynical. You have the right attitude.

Consulting specialists

When we concentrate our attention on that initial phase in decision making – establishing the truth – valuing is mixed in with all the other elements of thinking. You will be analysing and restructuring; you will be calling on your depth or subconscious mind for intuitions; you will be drawing heavily on your memory for relevant information or experience. But the valuing theme should be predominant.

By definition, almost, the top manager is a generalist. He may not understand all the complexities of advanced finance or all the mysteries of high technology. To do the 'establishing the truth' part he will have to consult others. In the theoretical world of management textbooks these specialists and staff advisers will give him the information upon which he can base his judgement. In practice, being human, they are all valuers too. They are offering him valuations – information plus a truth-judgement – just as surely as that expert at Christies who gave me a valuation on my telescope.

Your dependence on specialist help, together with valuing characteristics of those who must advise you mean that you have to become adept at another form of valuing, namely discovering if your advisers are telling you the truth. This is where educated intuition comes in. Once again people re-enter the stage of effective decision making.

In assessing the value of the information someone is giving you, you must gauge his calibre. You will always have at least a *little* knowledge about the matter in question, otherwise you would not be where you are. Use it to measure his greater knowledge. If there is an apparent conflict, sort it out. Do not be afraid to ask those questions which will indicate the length, depth, height and width of this person's knowledge. Do not make false assumptions about other people's expertise. Has this person been reliable in the past? Has he a reputation for honesty and integrity? Can you trust him to tell the truth, however unpalatable to you or himself?

Bad advisers will feed you interpretations of the situation which are far from objective or value-free. They want you to follow a particular course, and they feed you information to support their interpretation of reality. Conflicting evidence is put into the footnotes; other options are relegated to the appendices.

President Kennedy's decision in 1961 to countenance and support an invasion of Cuba by Cuban dissidents based in Florida – the Bay of Pigs affair – provides a classic example of how advisers with their own interests and objectives in mind can exercise a harmful influence on decision making. The body urging him to attempt the abortive invasion of Cuba by proxy – the Central Intelligence Agency – also happened to be the department supplying him with information about Cuba and the Cubans. You can guess what happened. This fact does not excuse Kennedy, of course. He had some knowledge from other sources, if only the newspapers. He should have made a judgement about the experts and the degree to which they could be expected to be impartial or disinterested. At least he learnt his lessons and dealt with the Cuban missile crisis far more effectively.

In consequence your first objective in any managerial position should be to place an absolute premium on the avoidance of error in your organisation. Sack those managers who play at party politicians, supplying you with suitably filtered or distorted information to support their policies. Redeploy those who cannot see the reality when it stares them in the face. Create an atmosphere of commitment to truth. Be willing to admit that you are wrong if the truth compels you to do so. By so doing you will set a good example.

Read the following example and then see if you can think of managers who exemplify this quality of truth-seeking in decision making, whether they are in the position of the chief executive (Churchill) or the specialist adviser (Jones).

The boffin who managed to bend the beam

Sir Winston Churchill always had a soft spot for the backroom boys. As Chancellor of the Exchequer in the 1920s he would summon Sir Ralph Hawtrey, the Treasury's financial and economic expert, with the instruction, according to his private secretary P.J. Grigg, that 'The learned man should be released from the dungeon in which we were said to have immured him, have his chains struck off and the straw brushed from his hair and clothes, and be admitted to the light and warmth of an argument in the Treasury boardroom with the greatest living master of argument.'

During his warlord period Sir Winston's favourite 'Boffin' was a young, softly spoken scientist called Dr R.V. Jones. The Prime Minister would spring him not from a Treasury basement but from 54 Broadway Buildings, the headquarters of MI6 across St James Park. The almost theological vendettas of grand scientist politicians like Lindemann and Tizard swiftly entered popular folklore after World War Two. The story of Reggie Jones, as he is known to his friends and contemporaries, had to wait until the 1970s for its full exposition when the most secret side of the war became public.

R.V. Jones made his great breakthrough on June 21, 1940. With his team at Broadway buildings he had been puzzling over radio beams transmitted from Germany during bomber raids over England. He became convinced they were a navigation device for steering aircraft to their targets. Some of the mighty were highly sceptical, refusing to believe that beams could be bent around the earth's surface. R.V. Jones believed they could, and what is more, that they could be bent again by counter measures in order to redirect the aerial raiders away from urban areas to drop their bombs over open country.

He entered his office that morning to find a message instructing him to come to the Cabinet Room at No 10. Suspecting revenge for a practical joke, he thought little of it but checked and found the message was genuine. He arrived 25 minutes late, Churchill asked him to elaborate a point of detail.

Instead he spoke for 20 minutes. 'The few minutes of desultory discussion that had ensued after my entry showed me that nobody else there knew as much about the matter as I did myself, and, although I was not conscious of my calmness at the time, the very gravity of the situation seemed to generate the steady nerve for which it called.'

Reg Jones made a lasting impression on the Prime Minister. Thereafter Churchill swore by him as 'the man who broke the bloody beam'; heady stuff for a 28-year-old. Churchill's support enabled him to beat the hierarchy on essential matters though, on one occasion, Sir Horace Wilson, head of the Civil Service, threatened to resign if Jones, a mere scientific officer, was awarded the CBE.

Like most members of the boffinry, R.V. Jones enjoyed a fight. In conversation recently at Aberdeen, where he continues to hold the chair of natural philosophy, he talked about his tactics in tackling scientists, soldiers and politicians more senior than himself: 'The first thing was to be absolutely scrupulous in trying to establish the truth. After the war Winston said: 'You don't have to be polite; you just have to be right.' If you got somebody, however eminent, and asked him three successive 'Why's?', there were not many people who could stand up to it. It was quite astonishing how shaky their basis was. It was the old story of 99 per cent perspiration and one per cent inspiration. One needed a very sound grounding in basic principles and a mistrust of elaborate argument when something simple would do.'[1]

The standard set by both Churchill and Jones – to be absolutely scrupulous in trying to establish the truth – is a high one and calls for teamwork in any organisation. But nothing less than attaining that standard should be your first aim if you seek excellence in management.

Valuing in perspective

Valuing is a general function of the mind: it is a dimension in all thinking rather than discrete function. But in certain mental situations we are conscious that it is playing the leading part, way ahead of analysing, synthesising or imagining. It may be most evident when you are acting as a judge, criticising someone casually or in trying to establish relative worth in a formal situation, such as interviewing a man or woman for a job. Judgement is our broad term for describing someone who is good at valuing as opposed to, say, the person who excels in logical thinking or having a fund of new ideas – not of course that these are mutually exclusive.

Because valuing is so general, I have concentrated in this chapter on the primacy of the truth-seeking form of valuing and your need to develop it by all means at your command. For establishing the truth – or the reality – of a situation seems to be the essential preliminary to knowing what is feasible. Decisions based on wishful thinking, false assumptions, undetected errors, careless calculations, faulty figures or vain assurances are hardly likely to succeed, except by luck.

A true leader will always speak the truth. For then his people will see the reality of their situation. Helping groups and organisations to do so and to respond appropriately lies at the very heart of leadership, especially in testing times. Consider this story.

La Vallete, the 72 year old Grand Master of the Knights of St John, who commanded Malta during the great siege by an immense force of Turks three centuries ago, was such a leader. Upon hearing news that there was no hope of an early relief he read the dispatch to his Council. 'We now know', Vallette said, 'that we must not look to others for our deliverance! It is only upon God and our own swords that we may rely. Yet this is no cause for us to be disheartened. Rather the opposite, for it is better to know the truth of one's situation than to be deceived by specious hopes'.

Surely La Vallete is right. But it is not always so easy to discover the truth of one's situation. The facts can be extremely complex, often distorted by others and apparently contradictory. This takes us to the mind's faculty for perceiving truth directly – intuition.

Reference

1   Hennessy, Peter. *Times Profile*, 13 March 1978.

8 Your sixth sense – intuition

What is intuition? How can you make better use of it? The aim of this chapter is to increase your awareness of the part played by intuition in decisions. Secondly, it will provide you with guidelines for making more effective use of your intuitive powers.

Intuition is the power or faculty of immediately apprehending that something is the case. Apparently it is done without intervention of any reasoning process. There is no deductive or inductive step-by-step reasoning, no conscious analysis of the situation, no employment of the imagination – just a quick and ready insight – 'I just know'.

'I have but a woman's reason', said one of Shakespeare's heroines. 'I think him so because I think him so'. Down the centuries women have been noted for their powers of intuition. Men have been counted as the more logical of the two sexes. Would you agree?

The object of intuition is usually truth in some form or other.

Therefore it is often a form of valuing done, if you like, without conscious effort and very quickly. The mind simply discerns the truth about a situation or a person, and that is it. Indeed, there is a tradition in philosophy known as intuitionalism, which holds that certain elements of knowledge – such as the fundamental principles of ethics – are based entirely upon intuition.

You recall that I suggested in the last chapter that we should distinguish between two phases in decision making:

- establishing the truth of the matter
- deciding what to do

The first process can be hard work. Sherlock Holmes personifies the thinker who relies primarily on looking carefully at the evidence and drawing correct deductions from the premises. That is one strategy. But the intuitive person does not seem to follow that route. His mind tells him instantly what must have happened or who committed the murder.

In practice it is not a question of either/or. A Sherlock Holmes may work logically for a time and then suddenly have an intuition, or conversely an intuitive person may be equipped with formidable powers of analysis which he habitually brings to bear upon his intuitions.

How intuitive are you?

Intuition is awareness that a situation exists when reason of logic – if consulted – might say that it was improbable or even impossible for it to do so. Do you have such awareness –

  rarely ☐   sometimes ☐
frequently ☐   never ☐

In your judgement of people do you tend to rely upon first impressions? Are they usually right?

Do you often 'feel' your way to a decision or to the solution of problems?

Do you find it difficult sometimes to explain your intuitions to others?

When your intuitions turn out to be wrong, by hindsight why is this so?

Managers are often deterred from recognising and using their own intuitive powers because they feel that, somehow, intuition is not intellectually respectable. It is certainly, they believe, not scientific enough. The cult of the rational manager has an iron grip on such minds. But this is nonsense. Some of the most celebrated scientists have been intuitive in their work. Some words by Einstein prove that point:

> There is no logical way to the discovery of these elemental laws. There is only the way of intuition, which is helped by a feeling for the order lying behind the appearance.

Trusting your intuition

If you are now inclined to be more aware and to give more status to intuition in thinking you have already taken the first step towards making better use of it. The next is to learn to trust your intuitive powers. That does not mean *always,* nor does it mean *occasionally,* because one cannot generalise about how often. But you should be prepared to give your intuition the benefit of the doubt; you should build up a warm and friendly relationship to that part of your mind which is prepared to offer you this unique service.

Intuition in practice

Read the following passage and consider the questions.

Mrs Golda Meir, former Israeli Prime Minister, once said she caused the initial debacle in the 1973 Yom Kippur war and ruined her political career, because she ignored her own intuition.

In her autobiography, the Russian-born and American-raised woman, who became Israel's Prime Minister, revealed that when, on Friday, 5 October, 1973, news was received that the Russian advisers were leaving Syria in a hurry, 'I tried not to become obsessive', she wrote. 'Besides, intuition is a very tricky thing. Sometimes it must be acted upon at once, but sometimes it is merely a symptom of anxiety'.

She was reassured by Moshe Dayan, then Minister of Defence,

the Chief of Staff and the Chief of Intelligence. They did not think war was imminent. Nor did General Bar Lev, former chief of staff.

She added: 'Today I know what I should have done. I should have overcome my hesitations that Friday morning. I should have listened to the warnings of my own heart and ordered a call-up. For me, that fact cannot and never will be erased and there can be no consolation in anything that anyone else has to say.'

Do you agree that Mrs Meir should have acted upon her intuition that Friday morning?

Can you identify an episode in your own life when you had an intuition which you failed to act upon? What were the consequences?

Emotion and intuition

'Sometimes it is merely a sympton of anxiety'. Emotion and intuition have their sources close together in the hinterland of the brain. It is quite possible for the wires to be crossed. The negative emotions of fear and anxiety can express themselves in intuitions. A nervous passenger may have an intuition that his flight to Paris will crash and he transfers to another one. The success rate in these anxiety intuitions is remarkably low. Positive emotions can also lead to wishful intuitions. A man or woman in love can have intuitions about the character of the adored lover which turn out to be groundless.

One implication is that a thinker who relies heavily upon intuition – as many really effective thinkers do – must be physically and emotionally fit. You only have to have a bad bout of influenza to know how it affects your emotions. You may become more irritable and more depressed; your focus of interest drops down to your tummy; you feel awful; you may be quite certain you are about to die. It is still remarkable, however, how many politicians and generals are allowed to make decisions when physically sick or mentally exhausted.

Stress and tiredness of mind or body can definitely play havoc with the intuitive thinker's immediate comprehension of the reality of a situation. Mountaineers are aware that decisions taken in a state of exhaustion drop dramatically in quality. If you are tired it is best to think logically what to do, and not to rely upon your intuition.

95

The classic example of the effects of emotional stress, physical sickness and plain tiredness upon an intuitive man is Adolf Hitler. He possessed considerable flair as a politician and as a military leader. His decision to invade France through the Ardennes was based on an intuition of the truth in contrast to the more logical thinking of his opponents and even his own highly rational General Staff. But, by 1945, the effects of war had reduced him to a shadow of his former self. Stress symptoms, such as hand trembling and face twitches, were visible to all. As he disliked bad news he surrounded himself with men who filtered information for him. Bad news was dressed up as good news. Gradually Hitler lost contact with reality and retreated more into a private world, symbolised by the underground *führerbunker* of his last weeks. Disturbed by stress and emotion, fed with misleading information, his intuition had become a worthless instrument.

Business flair

'Looking back on my own scientific work', said Lord Adrian, a Nobel Prize Winner and a President of the Royal Society, 'I

ffolkes

"The latest theory is that business acumen is a virus."

should say that it shows no great originality but a certain amount of business instinct which leads to the selection of a profitable line'.

Instinct, flair and intuition are really much the same. A person who consistently deploys an instinctive power of discernment in a certain field is said to have flair. He can 'smell' a good prospect or in what direction the truth might lie; rather than reasoning towards his goal step-by-step he sniffs his way there by intuition. Indeed flair comes from a French verb meaning to smell.

'When I first started drilling in the Oklahoma oil fields,' wrote J. Paul Getty, 'the consensus of expert judgement held that there could be no oil in the so-called Red Beds region. But like so many oilmen, I chose to temper all "analytical" thinking with a healthy dose of non-logical subjectivity. To me, the area looked as if it might hide oil. Largely on the basis of a hunch, I decided to see for myself. I began drilling in the Red Beds, struck oil and brought in a vast new producing field. I rather suspect that by relying upon such nontextbook thought processes and taking attendant risks, the biggest fortunes have been made – in oil and other endeavours.'

Business flair is a consistent theme in the lives of great industrialists and merchants. They intuitively spot an opportunity for making money. They can smell a potential profit where others can see nothing but present losses. It is an instinct apart from the dictates of reason or logic which guide more plodding minds. When it is not followed, such businessmen frequently find out later their mistake, just as Golda Meir did.

If you add to this kind of business flair, the willingness to take risks in the employment of capital, you are dealing with an entrepreneur. An entrepreneur can be a one-man operator of course, but more often than not he sets up a company. He organises. He becomes in effect a manager or at least an employer of managers whom he hires to run his business. But despite his gifts of intuition in business situations he might not be at all so intuitive about people. For nature rarely bestows all its mental talents on one man.

The career of Henry Ford (1863–1947) provides an interesting case study of a thinker with an unusual combination of intuitive strengths. As a man he was stubborn, hard to persuade and erratic. A farmer's son in Michigan, Ford eventually achieved his goal and produced a car for the masses.

Ford had little formal education and as a result he had difficulty in both reading and writing. He had a natural mechanical aptitude which manifested itself early on when he repaired and serviced his father's farm machinery. The arrival of the first American automobile fired his imagination and he set himself the objective of producing a motor car. This he achieved after seven years of toil – all in his leisure time. Ford was not a brilliant mechanic, but he possessed aptitude and burning ambition, hardworking capability and an interest in innovation.

Ford's first car, produced in 1896 when he was part owner and chief engineer of the Detroit Auto Company, proved to be a commercial failure. He was undaunted, however, and started to develop a motor car which people in their thousands would want to buy. This unique intuition was the key to Ford's success. He saw a whole brand new market for mass transport. This concept, and the determination to be 'first with the most' drove him on. It was indicative of his mind that he determined to travel down one path to the exclusion of all others. There was no pretence at being a broad thinker.

Ford was exceptionally weak in face-to-face encounters and went out of his way to avoid such confrontations. Decisions affecting his senior executives, often controversial, were never discussed. He never told people why they were fired, his totally intuitive approach often seemed at odds with reason. There is some inconsistency in his concern, on the one hand, for paying high wages, and yet on the other, his disregard for personal feelings if his intuition told him to do something. It was impossible to understand Ford in a logical way; he was a man who had to be sensed.

This intuitive approach did, however, provide Ford with one of his greatest strengths – his ability to detect the strengths and weaknesses of people and consequently his ability to form and re-form the team around him. It was this almost perpetual revolution which he generated which kept the Ford Motor Company active. He never allowed people to get on terms with the job because he felt that this would stifle creativity. This style kept the industry in perpetual ferment but kept it fresh with change.

By the early 1920s the Ford Motor Company was the world's

biggest company, with huge cash reserves even by today's standards. By the end of that decade, though, Ford was unprofitable and uncompetitive and it stayed that way until Henry Ford's grandson Henry Ford II took over in 1944. The reasons for the dramatic decline are many: General Motors was a main cause in the market place. But the whole Ford story had become a controlled experiment in mismanagement. Henry Ford's empire almost died because his style, so right in the early days, was not appropriate when the company became a giant. Henry Ford was the 'boss'; he gave the orders, took all the decisions and his subordinates were simply not allowed to think for themselves or to manage.

Conclusion

Far from being a marginal and out-dated endowment, as the rational manager believes, intuition is central to the way successful thinkers work. For the natural or applied scientist, it is the apparently unconscious ability which some have to pick out from various possibilities the actual way in which a process does or could work; or it may be an early recognition from below the conscious level, that one is on the right track; or again it may be the flair to select problems or lines of enquiry which are both important and soluble. These results matter equally to the manager in his field. Therefore encourage intuition in yourself. Become more aware of it. Be more receptive to its often faint whisper. Always subject them, however, to evaluation. Granted that safeguard, intuition can save you a great deal of time in decision making.

Reference

1   Meir, Golda, *My Life*, Weidenfeld and Nicholson, 1975.

9 Your depth mind

The previous chapter on intuition highlighted the importance of the depth or unconscious mind's part in thinking. This chapter continues on that theme, specifically relating it to business decisions. It has the specific objective of helping you to make better use of what might be called your mental computer.

Have you recently had the experience of locking up your house and setting out on a journey, only to remember after a mile or two that you have left a light on, or a window open, or forgotten some vital piece of paper? Most of us do. We call it memory, but it is not the same sort of memory we rack when trying to recall someone's name when asked or, say, the name of some product which is now unavailable.

If you think about it, your mental computer must scan and process an enormous amount of information before it prints up for you that simple message: 'you have left the bathroom light on'. That may be why it takes its time.

There is learning at work here too. For the fact that you have left the bathroom light on two or three times is fed into your computer. Before leaving the house on a future occasion your depth mind may prompt you: 'better just check the lights again'. That is experience.

Using the principle

The main characteristic, then, of the depth mind in relation to decisions is that it tends to work *after* the decision. It is only when the suitcase is actually packed and in the back of the car that you remember you have left out your toothbrush.

In decisions involving moral values – right and wrong, good and bad, we call this reviewing of decisions after the event *conscience*. 'That was wrong', says the computer in the guise of conscience. Valuing often works backwards in this way, especially where the self is concerned.

This annoying characteristic of the subconscious mind is most inconvenient for the decision maker. You want your depth mind to do its work for you *before* you are irrevocably committed.

This is where the *point of no return* concept becomes significant. Literally, it is the position on a flight where the pilot must go on if he is in trouble rather than turn back home. By extension, it means that point in time after you have decided you cannot change your mind. This of course is rarely one position: there is usually a continuum of points, with the costs of changing your mind escalating as you proceed down it. For decisions soon begin to set hard, like cement. Despite that scale or continuum, it is useful to try to identify *your* point of no return.

By design or accident then decisions tend to have what could be compared to an engagement period before marriage. You have proposed and been accepted, the decision made. You are engaged but not actually married. The decision has yet to be fully implemented. The wedding ceremony should be your point of no return – 'for better or worse, for richer or poorer, in sickness or in health'.

During that engagement period in any decision, provided you are acting in good faith, your depth mind may well say: 'this isn't

101

right for you'. You may have to distinguish that voice from the pressures of other people or the natural cold feet of anyone facing a vital decision. Do you recall the point I made earlier, namely that anxiety can distort both one's judgement and one's intuition?

Once hotelman Conrad Hilton was trying to buy an old hotel in Chicago whose owners promised to sell to the highest bidder. Several days before the deadline date for sealed bids Hilton submitted a hastily made 165,000 dollar offer. He went to bed that night feeling vaguely disturbed and woke next morning with a hunch that his bid was not high enough. 'That didn't feel right to me', he later wrote. 'Another figure kept coming, 180,000 dollars. It satisfied me. It seemed fair. It felt right. I changed my bid to the larger figure on that hunch. When they were opened the closest bid to mine was 179,000 dollars'.[1]

Can you think of a similar incident in your career so far?

Hilton was fortunate in that he still had time to change his decision. Nor was he hooked on the notion that once you have made a decision it shows want of character to change your mind. It may do *after* your point of no return, but not *before* it. 'A wise man changes his mind, a fool never.'

It has been discovered that any decision will prod the depth mind into action. You flip a coin between a holiday in France and one in Spain. 'Heads it's France', you conclude firmly. A few hours later you know beyond a shred of doubt that you really want to go to Spain. Providing you have not booked your tickets irrevocably, change your mind!

By making a conscious effort to review experience you can develop your depth mind into a formidable instrument. Trusting it is important. Also you should develop a special kind of inward sensitivity, so that you can pick up the delicate signals, that thought which stirs imperceptibly, like a leaf touched by the air, telling you that something is moving. As Conrad Hilton writes: 'I know when I have a problem and have done all I can to figure it, I keep listening in a sort of inside silence until something clicks and I feel a right answer'.

For the best descriptions of the depth mind at work in business decisions we turn again to Lord Thomson. In his autobiography *After I was Sixty* (1975), he mused upon the impulses and skills that led him to pursue with great success his distinguished business career long after most of us have retired:

I must now ask myself: what was it that gave me this self-confidence, this determination and adventurous spirit in business . . . at 67?

It was at least partly due to my discovery over a fairly long period, but more than ever during these latter years in Edinburgh and London, that experience was a very important element in the management side of business and it was, of course, the one thing that I had plenty of. I could go further and say that for management to be good it generally must be experienced. To be good at anything at all requires a lot of practice, and to be really good at taking decisions you have to have plenty of practice at taking decisions. The more one is exposed to the necessity of making decisions, the better one's decision-making becomes.

At various times during my business life I have had to take some important decisions and, particularly in the early days, I often got these wrong. But I found later that the early mistakes and, for that matter, the early correct decisions stood me in good stead. Most of the problems that I was confronted with in London were in one way or another related to those earlier ones. It was often a matter of just adding some zeros to figures and the sums were the same. In a great many instances I knew the answer immediately.

I cannot explain this scientifically, but I was entirely convinced that, through the years, in my brain as in a computer, I had stored details of the problems themselves, the decisions reached and the results obtained; everything was neatly filed away there for future use. Then, later, when a new problem arose, I would think it over and, if the answer was not immediately apparent, I would let it go for a while, and it was as if it went the rounds of the brain cells looking for guidance that could be retrieved, for by next morning, when I examined the problem again, more often than not the solution came up right away. That judgement seemed to be come to almost unconsciously, and my conviction is that during the time I was not consciously considering the problem, my subconscious had been turning it over and relating it to my memory; it had been held up to the light of the experiences I had had in past years, and the way through the difficulties became obvious. I am pretty sure other older men have had this same evidence of the brain's subconscious work.

This makes it all very easy, you may say. But, of course, it doesn't happen easily. That bank of experience from which I was able to draw in the later years was not easily funded.

The International Business Machines Company – one of the world's great business organisations – have had for many years a single word as their motto. A sign over every executive's desk spells it out: 'Think'. Let us be honest with ourselves and consider how averse we all are to doing just that. Thinking is work. In the early stages of a man's career it is very hard work. When a difficult decision or problem arises, how easy it is, after looking at it superficially, to give up thinking about it. It is easy to put it from one's mind. It is easy to decide that it is insoluble, or that something will turn up to help us. Sloppy and inconclusive thinking becomes a habit. The more one does it the more one is unfitted to think a problem through to a proper conclusion.

If I have any advice to pass on, as a successful man, it is this: if one wants to be successful, one must think; one must think until it hurts. One must worry a problem in one's mind until it seems there cannot be another aspect of it that hasn't been considered. Believe me, that is hard work and, from my close observation, I can say that there are few people indeed who are prepared to perform this arduous and tiring work. But let me go further and assure you of this: while, in the early stages, it is hard work and one must accept it as such, later one will find that it is not so difficult, the thinking apparatus has become trained; it is trained even to do some of the thinking subconsciously as I have shown. The pressure that one had to use on one's poor brain in the early stages no longer is necessary; the hard grind is rarely needed; one's mental computer arrives at decisions instantly or during a period when the brain seems to be resting. It is only the rare and most complex problems that require the hard toil of protracted mental effort.

By chance I happened to be reading Eugen Herrigel's *Zen in the Art of Archery* at the same time as Thomson's book. It is an account published in 1953 by a young German philosopher, the first European to go to Japan in order to understand Zen. To that end he studied archery under a great master named Kenzo Awa for over five years, practising endlessly the various techniques of drawing the bow. But he learnt that to master an art, technical knowledge is not enough. Technique has to be transcended; the art has to grow naturally out of the unconscious. Zen is clearly holistic; it places much emphasis on the depth mind. As conscious analysis and calculation recede, the archer allows his depth mind to think and decide for him. The shot 'falls' from the bow like a ripe fruit from the bough. Thomson is really saying much the same about business decision making. Both the master archer and the master businessman make it look simple, but years of thought and practice lie behind their easy skills.

Some guidelines

For a long time we have known that the unconscious mind plays a strategic role in creative thinking, but the part it plays in the decisions of experienced managers is new territory which I have opened up in this book. You should have picked up the following points from Lord Thomson's advice for more reflection and action:

- *The way to become good at decision making is to make lots of decisions in your field*
  Practice makes perfect. That proverb will apply to decision making if practice is based upon sound principles.
- *See relations between your decisions, despite differences of time, place and scale*
  Thomson saw connections between the problems he faced in Canada and those he encountered in London. Those earlier decisions, correct and incorrect, were in the computer: 'In a great many instances I knew the answer immediately'.
- *Look on your brain as a mental computer*
  Earlier sequences of decisions and results are fed into the mind. Where solutions are not easily apparent, allow time for your depth mind to work on it. As a principle, a period of close enquiry and reflection should be followed either by a change of subject or a period of inactivity.
- *Shun mental laziness*
  At all stages of your career conscious thinking demands some very hard work. You have to be prepared for that effort. If you do it when young you reap the benefit of an exceptionally good depth mind.

105

- *Few people are willing to make the effort*
  That is a challenging comment. It could be good news for you. As the proverb says, 'The many fail, the one succeeds'.

Reference

1   Hilton, Conrad N., *Be my Guest*, Prentice-Hall, 1957.

10 Options

In this chapter you will read about the second important aspect of decision making or problem solving. Having established the truth to the best of your ability, you are then in a position to generate and choose between possible courses of action or solutions, called here *options*. By the end of it you should have a clear idea of the structure of options and know how to manage the process of selecting from them the best one for your purpose.

It was 17 September, 1862. Cannon thundered along the battle lines as two armies of Blue and Grey soldiers faced each other across the Antietam Creek. Then General Ambrose Burnside gave order to advance. The Union army was to storm across the creek and attack the enemy at close quarters. The route he chose to send them led over the narrow bridge across the creek, the only one in the vicinity. The Confederate gunners in the batteries specially placed to command the bridge could hardly believe their eyes. They swept away regiment after regiment with grapeshot. The slaughter was appalling.

General Burnside had failed to discover that the Antietam Creek in this region was only about three feet deep. It could have been forded by infantry or cavalry at any point with perfect safety. Of the battle at Antietam and the general who lost it for him President Lincoln said somewhat bitterly: 'Only he could have wrung so spectacular a defeat from the jaws of victory'.

Burnside had acted on the assumption that he had only one option open to him. In fact we now know that he was wrong. He had not carried out a thorough reconnaissance. His decision rested upon an erroneous understanding of his situation.

In the same way, business histories are full of disasters which came about because all the options were not considered. We cannot put the price up; we cannot risk a strike; we cannot possibly afford a 5 per cent increase in wages, are all examples of

"It was precisely this kind of indecisiveness that got us into trouble in the first place!"

refusal to consider a particularly unpleasant option. It may, however, not even be an unpleasant option that is ignored; 'I never thought of *that*' is an all too common cry.

Considering options is inseparable from gathering information about the situation. As you scan a situation, analysing and sifting it, you will see the more obvious possibilities for action. In the second phase of thinking, when you have grasped the essentials of the problem or situation, you switch your mental forces to a new front: reviewing and perhaps adding to that list of possibilities.

Developing a range of options

It is important in this phase to understand what you are seeking. You are not seeking *all* the possibilities of action. That step, so often recommended in management textbooks, is a recipe for indecision. Take chess. You might assume that a computer can look at every possible move in the game. That is not so. A very ordinary game will run to 25 moves, and if a computer wants to consider every possibility equally, it has to consider one thousand million, million, million, etc. (1 followed by 75 zeros) combinations of moves.

Suppose computers could consider a million moves a second, which they cannot do yet, it would take many millions of times longer than the entire history of our planetary system for them to sort out all the possibilities. Therefore a computer, like you or me, looks only a few moves ahead. In this activity a computer's weakness lies in its absence of a valuing faculty. The chess master knows at once which moves are *feasible,* and that means worth considering.

That word *feasible* is crucially important because it saves you time. When it comes to scanning options it helps immeasurably if you know what you are looking for. What is *possible* is a much wider term. It embraces everything that could be done within the limits of the situation. Whereas *feasible* narrows it down a little to *what can be done with existing resources.*

You remember that logicians analyse syllogisms by reducing them to a skeleton and lettering the parts, so that they can see

109

more clearly their relations? I shall employ much the same principle here.

The first task to perform is to sort out the feasible options from the greater number of possible options. Imagine yourself as a coin dealer or a diamond merchant sifting quickly through someone's collection and choosing the five or six specimens that are worth considering for purchase.

Then you proceed by *elimination*. So the process resembles a cone: as shown in Fig. 10.1.

It is common sense, as well as scientific orthodoxy now, that it is easier to disprove things than to prove them. Theoretically you cannot prove anything finally and conclusively, but for practical purposes you can, so far as your approximation to truth is near enough for everyday needs. Science is constantly trying to devise tests to support or disprove hypotheses. All that a truthful scientist can say about a hypothesis is that it has survived all those tests up to this date.

As Einstein replied to a lady who was congratulating him on news of an astronomical observation that seemed to prove his theory of relativity: 'Madam, a thousand experiments cannot ever prove me right; a single experiment can prove me wrong'.

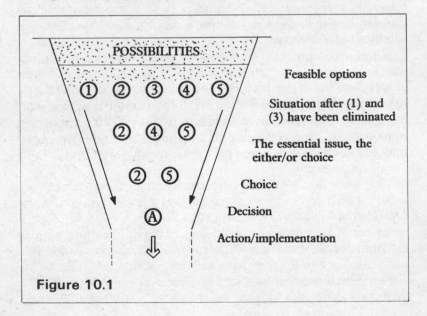

Figure 10.1

110

Your object in working on the feasible options is to reduce them to two alternatives – *either* this *or* that – as soon as possible. But remember the proverb: 'More haste, less speed'.

Alternatives, in the strict sense, are mutually exclusive. To marry either Mary or Jane is an alternative: in our society you cannot marry both. The first thing to do is check if the alternatives are truly alternative. After all, they may not have survived the mental obstacle course you have created for them unless you liked them both. If, in fact, they are not attractive – if they are the two 'least worst' options – you may be pleased to drop one of them. But these are situations when you can opt for both of them, possibly in sequence – the 'trial-and-error' method. Or you can combine, mix or blend them in some other way.

The do-nothing option is sometimes worth considering

If neither alternative attracts you, and if you cannot produce a satisfactory compromise, it is always worth asking yourself, 'Do I have to take action at all?' The option of doing nothing, of deciding not to act, is always worth considering. Sometimes the proposed cure promises to be worse than the disease, but the decision to do nothing must be taken for a very good reason and not because you cannot think of another way.

As a variation, if there is no obvious winner, nor a trade-off between objective achievement and implementability, you may want to choose the option which is most likely to keep your options open. The strategy of keeping options open for as long as possible has much to commend it.

Option check-list

Constantly ask yourself and your colleagues these questions:

● Which possibilities are feasible, given our limitations?
● Which of the feasible options are the true alternatives?

111

- Are they mutually exclusive, or can we do
  (a) both or
  (b) some creative combination of the two?
- Will the resulting compromise achieve our objective better than either of the discrete courses?
- Would it be better to do nothing?
- In what circumstances should we abandon the policy of keeping our options open for as long as possible?

You may object that there often is not time to work steadily through the cone. But even in the most tense situations it is best to keep your head and mentally check out the most likely possibilities.

An option problem

You are the engineer on flight BA 507 en route from London to Caracas. At 30,000 feet all four engines stop for no apparent reason. What do you do?
  (a) guess the cause and work on that
  (b) work through the standard checklist
You choose (b). Having completed the checklist you still have not found the cause of engine failure. You are now at 8000 feet. What do you do next? Send out distress signals? Fix parachutes?
(You have one minute from now to answer this question. Turn to p. 173 for the answer when you have jotted yours down.)

Intuitive thinkers tend to jump to the either-or situation without apparently going through a conscious process of eliminating alternatives. Albert Speer, one of Hitler's intimates, noted this tendency. His close associates even joked openly about it to Hitler's face, without him taking offence. Thus his standard phrase, 'There are two possibilities', would be used by one of his secretaries, in his presence, often in the most everyday context. She would say: 'There are two possibilities. Either it is going to rain or it is not going to rain'.

Hitler's failure to think systematically about military situations, compounded by a growing distrust of those generals and staff officers around him who could, plus the effects of stress upon his undoubted natural flair as a commander, lost him the Second World War.

112

False assumptions: some examples from history

Once you have acquired some knowledge about the apparent limits or limitations in a problem or situation, you should test them for reality. This is value thinking: are they real or true limits, or are they false ones. This may require some physical work. Had he carried out a proper reconnaissance, General Burnside would have discovered that Antietam Creek was not a real limitation to the movement of soldiers. Far from being a boundary, it was an open gateway.

Military history abounds with examples of generals exploiting the infinite capacity of the human mind to make false assumptions about limits. Before his invasion of Italy early in his career Napoleon read many writers who repeated that it was impracticable to consider crossing the Alps in winter with a large army. His staff officers agreed. But Napoleon always thought for himself, and he challenged that view:

> 'The winter is not the most unfavourable season for the passage of lofty mountains', he said. 'The snow is then firm, the weather settled, and there is nothing to fear from avalanches, the real and only danger to be apprehended in the Alps. On those high mountains, there are often very fine days in December, of a dry cold, with extreme calmness in the air'.

Hitler made a similar decision in 1940, when he brushed aside the received conclusion of the German General Staff that it would be impossible to take armoured divisions through the wooded hills of the Ardennes – and was proved to be right.

In the 1930s the British Imperial General Staff spent much time resolving how to defend Britain's colonies in the Far East. They fortified the island of Singapore as a bastion, constructing powerful batteries of heavy guns to make it impregnable from the sea and a great naval base to shelter the fleet which would be sent there in war time. Little time was spent on the possibility that Singapore would be attacked by land across the causeway which joined it to the mainland. The British military planners assumed that the mountainous jungle of Malaya was impassable to a

113

modern army. Nor did they spend much money on air defences, for the admirals were convinced that aircraft could not pose much threat to warships.

In 1941 the plan was put into action. Two battleships, the *Prince of Wales* and the *Repulse* were despatched to the Far East to overawe the Japanese. To the surprise of the British generals, however, the Japanese did not obligingly land in front of the British guns but in the north on the mainland. The two British battleships sailed to intercept the invasion fleet but were both sunk by Japanese aircraft. The Japanese struck south through the jungle with ease, and attacked Singapore from the landward side. As the large guns were all pointing the wrong way the city fell within days and 10,000 British and Australian soldiers became prisoners. In Churchill's words it was 'the largest capitulation in British history'.

Again, the business world is full of companies that made false assumptions about limits. The Japanese 'invasion' of the British motor cycle industry provides an example: the British motor cycle firms assumed that the only competition was amongst themselves.

Some limitations affecting management choices

Knowing where to look for limitations will save time. Here are four suggested key areas where care should be taken to establish the real limits in a given situation.

Time

Perhaps the first question you should ask in any decision making situation is, 'How much time have we got?' Is that the real amount of time? Why is it not more – or less? Test the limit, especially if someone else is laying down a time scale for you. They may be making a false assumption about how much time is available. Many problems can be solved if we adopt a longer time scale for their solution. But that requires patience – a management quality often in short supply.

Information

No decision maker ever has all the information he needs. Again there has to be a judgement at some point. For the quest for information is subject to the law of diminishing returns. At first you gain a great deal of information in a short space of time; gradually you are spending more-and-more time and effort to acquire what is in effect less-and-less relevant information. The real limit is the point in a given situation where you judge that the cost in time and money of obtaining more information becomes too high.

Resources

There will be a variety of resources, but the obvious ones for a businessman include the amount of money you have available. You should remember the 'opportunity cost': if you use your resources for this purpose you will be detracting from your resources elsewhere; in other words, you will make a limitation for yourself in another sector. Machinery is another resource. It is no good promising a customer a thousand a week at once if you machines can only produce half that number.

Knowledge

If you study successes and failures in business diversification one factor stands out: the knowledge of managers. That embraces both knowledge of the business field in question and knowledge of management – including leadership, decision making and communication. If your managers are limited numbers in experience and in quality, then that sets a limit upon what you can attempt.

Generating more options

Decision implies real choice. The more feasible options within the broad constraints of time and space you have to choose from the better your decision is likely to be.

115

Even if there appears to be one course open once the truth has been established an experienced manager will cast around in his mind to see if there is not another option. By closing thought down too early, good option can be the enemy of the best option.

Here imaginative thinking comes into its own. We must draw a sharp distinction between *unconscious* assumptions (which may, of course, be true or untrue) and the *conscious* assumptions or suppositions which we can use as a portable step-ladder in imaginative thinking.

Supposing we had an extra million pounds, what would we do then?

Let us *assume* that the trade union will not object to this plan, how would we implement it?

Assuming, for the moment, that the Board agrees ...

Imagination can sometimes be employed to construct assumptions in order to test others.

Looking back on that abortive invasion of Cuba – the Bay of Pigs fiasco – mentioned in a previous chapter the then Secretary of State, Dean Rusk, recalled that President Kennedy had conceived a totally unrealistic idea of what a puny brigade of Cuban exiles could possibly achieve. 'I should have told the President', said Rusk, 'that we *might* want to do it with American forces. 'Ask your military chiefs of staff', I should have said to him, 'to assume that American troops would be used. Then get them to tell you what they must have before they invaded Cuba – what air support, ground divisions and naval back-up. If we had made that assumption we should never have made such an error'.

Creative imagination comes more into play, however, when you are thinking about how to use existing resources. Your mind can easily become dominated by what some psychologists have called *functional fixedness,* the tendency to see things in association with a given function. The conventional mind accepts these sorts of assumptions: a hammer is for hammering in nails, an army camp is for housing soldiers – if there are no more soldiers, knock it down. Children, before they acquire functional fixedness, are much more imaginative in their play. An object for them can take on any number of uses. The way holiday camps came into being provides an excellent example of creative imagination at work:

Billy Butlin was a circus man. When he looked over disused army camps in 1946 he conceived the idea of using them as holiday camps. He even kept the army's tannoy system which he found in the camps. He was told it wouldn't work, but Butlin's Holiday Camps played a major part in meeting the needs of the British people, especially before the era of cheap overseas holiday packages.

In imaginative thinking intended to overcome functional fixedness it is useful to remember the principle of artificially restraining or disciplining the critical, analytical, reasoning function. Make the analysers wait their turn. Let your mind off its habitual leashes so that it roams freely wherever it wills to go in the field you have chosen.

There are two kinds of people when it comes to trying to think about fresh possibilities. The first, when confronted with a new idea, will react in a distinctly negative way. By clear, logical thinking he may soon be able to show that the idea is wrong or that the plan is unworkable. The second type will react differently. He toys with it, and speculates what the implications might be if they could be demonstrated. Because of the novelty of the proposal his impulse is to wish it could be shown to be true.

A condition of creativity seems to be a readiness to side with, to empathize with and explore the possibilities of fresh ideas. It also seems to be compatible with the attitude of discriminating criticism previously discussed. The attitude consists, in fact, of vigorous attention to ideas which, because they are important, merit criticism in the interests of their refinement or extension.

The principle of *suspending judgement,* as it is called, lies at the heart of the popular technique of brainstorming. Here the evaluation of ideas is deliberately kept at bay until a sufficient number have been produced by the free-wheeling processes of thought. But the barrier erected by premature criticism in creative thinking was recognised long before 1927, the year when Alex Osborn invented brainstorming. Johann Schiller, the celebrated German poet who trained as a lawyer, then became a

117

military surgeon and ended his career as professor of history at Jena in 1788, wrote to a friend:

> The reason for your complaint (about not being creative) lies, it seems to me, in the constraint which your intellect imposes upon your imagination. Here I will make an observation, and illustrate it by an allegory. Apparently, it is not good – and indeed it hinders the creative work of the mind – if the intellect examines too closely the ideas already pouring in, as it were, at the gates. Regarded in isolation, an idea may be quite insignificant, and venturesome in the extreme, but it may acquire importance from an idea which follows it; perhaps in a certain collocation with other ideas, which may seem equally absurd, it may be capable of furnishing a very serviceable link. The intellect cannot judge all those ideas unless it can retain them until it has considered them in connection with these other ideas. In the case of a creative mind, it seems to me, the intellect has withdrawn its watchers from the gates, and the ideas rush in pell-mell, and only then does it review and inspect the multitude. You worthy critics, or whatever you may call yourselves, are ashamed or afraid of the momentary and passing madness which is found in all real creators, the longer or shorter duration of which distinguishes the thinking artist from the dreamer. Hence your complaints of unfruitfulness, for you reject too soon and discriminate too severely.[1]

Although either may be premature, it is always useful to bear in mind the distinction between negative and constructive criticism. The negative critic is like an underwater fisherman equipped with a gun and various darts – killer phrases which he launches at any fish he sees stirring in your depth mind, such as:

- We tried that before
- Let's get back to reality
- I don't like the idea
- Good idea in theory – but impracticable
- You'll make us a laughing stock
- Where did you dig that one up from?
- It's never been tried before
- It will not work here
- It cannot be done
- We've always done it this way
- Costs too much

118

A true critic might be defined as one who expresses a reasoned opinion on any matter involving a judgement of its *value,* such as truth, beauty or technical quality. He appreciates what value is there. The constructive part comes into play when such a critic suggests ways in which value can be added to the idea or matter under scrutiny.

Assessing the consequences

The game of consequences lies at the heart of the rational approach to decision making. But consequences, when you examine them carefully are not susceptible to precise calculation.

As a principle, the more familiar a situation is to you the more you can judge consequences. Or someone else's experience may give you clues, which is why history is so important. The newer the situation, as a corollary, the less likely you are to be able to predict consequences.

Now all situations are partly old or familiar (at least to someone else if not to you), and partly unique. History both does and does not repeat itself. You can see how difficult it then becomes to predict outcomes.

In 1965 the Americans decided to mount a strategic bombing offensive against the North Vietnamese forces. Therefore they had to build airbases near Saigon in the south. To protect these bases they sent 3000 marines. But the US Marine Corps is trained to be aggressive. Rather than sit around their perimeters the commanders on the ground decided on a policy of active defence and defined their objective in terms of killing the Vietcong. Soon more soldiers had to be transported there to support them. And more. And more.

Slipshod thinking of this kind about consequences is all too common. After such events the argument becomes a matter of historical judgement: could the Americans have foreseen such results and also, ought they to have done so. These are questions of responsibility and blame, involving our powers to make some often very fine distinctions between reasons and excuses. It is better to think thoroughly about possible and probable consequences in advance: the more of them that can be identified the better.

The importance of probability

There is a danger that the more your mind unravels possible consequences the less likely you are to do anything. Fortunately for us, we cannot foresee all the manifest and latent consequences of all the options open to us at any one time: we have to take some sort of a risk. In business decisions it is usually the case that the larger the risk the greater is the potential gain. That principle is always worth bearing in mind. Risk taking seems to be inseparable from decision making. What are the guidelines?

The chief principle is that risks should be taken only after being carefully calculated. That means a very thorough effort, using the imagination as well as all the methods of quantification that are relevant, to calculate as precisely as possible the nature and degree of the risks involved. Then you are in a position to see what can be done to minimise the risks by prudent foresight and contingency planning. Paul Getty once said: 'When I go into any business deal my chief thoughts are on how I'm going to save myself if things go wrong'.

The proposed benefits should warrant the risk. A successful investment banker, for example, will have ensured that on his ventures of capital, the upside potential for him is far in excess of the downside risk. If he gets it right on any given proposition his investment and bank will make many times its original stake. Even if an investment is a complete failure, providing he has exercised proper care, the bank should still lose no more than the money it invested. The critical factor is always to get the odds right on each investment and only to invest when the upside potential is high in relation to the initial sum advanced.

Knowing that you can accept the precisely predicted consequences of failure is a sign that you have properly explored the risk element of a decision. Ask yourself what is the worst possible outcome? Am I prepared to accept it if necessary? Both asking and answering those two questions will greatly ease the task of making a difficult decision.

The various systematic ways of exploring the outcomes of alternative courses of action, using diagrams and mathematical calculations of the odds, are taught in business schools. But I doubt if more than one in ten managers ever makes use of them in work situations. Yet the principle of exploring probabilities as far as possible is sound. These days the exploration of the probabilities of each outcome can be greatly aided by computers in many cases. But computers can never make up your mind. Remember that you are always dealing with *estimated* probabilities. Therefore results will depend on how good you are at that form of judgement. Even where genuine doubts about estimates exist, however, it is at least useful to be able to examine them as thoroughly as possible.

Summary

At the core of making decisions lies the activity of collecting, assessing and choosing from a set of options. If there is genuinely only one course of action open, there is hardly a decision to be made. The options considered should be feasible. It is useful to aim to reduce the list systemmatically by a process of elimination until you are left with the two alternatives. The more relevant information you can gather both before and during this process, the easier it will be.

When considering options the chief enemy of effective decision making is entertaining false assumptions about either your own limitations or those of your competitors. You have to be objective about what you have at your disposal: time, knowledge, resources and knowledge. Always be ruthless about the true facts of the case.

This thinking – partly analytical, partly valuing – should give way to creative thinking if it is felt necessary to generate some new options. Here you and your colleagues need to be able to suspend judgement, so that the dogs of criticism do not tear every new born idea to shreds.

Even the most original idea or course of action, however, will have predictable consequences which have to be explored in as objective a way as possible. Indeed the rational way to make decisions is to assess options by weighing their outcomes, both in the short term and in the longer term perspective. Desired outcomes are so because they realise the purpose, aims and objectives of the organisation.

Risk is a dimension in many decisions, not least in business life. Risks have to be carefully calculated. Computers can aid managers in a growing number of instances but they should still be seen as auxilliaries to human judgement. When considering the benefits of a risk, attention must be given to the consequences of incurring the loss or danger which is at the heart of the risk. Commitment control – or the ability and willingness to say no – is vital. The assessment of probability can give you guidance what to do. As Cicero said, 'Probabilities guide the decisions of wise men'.

Reference

1   Brill, A.A. (ed.), *The Basic Writings of Sigmund Freud*, Random House, 1938.

11 Arguing

'Gentlemen, I take it we are all in complete agreement on the decision here'. Alfred P. Sloan, the head of General Motors, looked around the committee room table. His senior managers nodded in assent. 'Then', continued Sloan, 'I propose we postpone further discussion of this matter until our next meeting to give ourselves time to develop disagreement and perhaps gain some understanding of what the decision is about'.

Several centuries earlier Shakespeare had expressed the same truth in a sentence: 'Rightly to be great is not to stir without great argument'. By 'great argument' Shakespeare meant a debate of high quality upon the reasons for and against the various courses of action. That is just what Sloan had sensed was lacking in his committee.

Personal ways of thinking it out with others vary considerably. Some managers favour an argumentative style. Take Lord Thomson again. On one occasion, which must have been typical of many, Thomson took one of his senior executives, Gordon Brunton, with him to Scotland to clinch a deal.

I recall that two days after he got back, I had him on the plane with me bound for Edinburgh and another deal, and the two of us arguing all the way north about how we should handle it. We were going to make an offer to Thomas Nelson and Sons, no less, to take over their considerable business in educational and other books. Gordon and I were arguing all the way to Turnhouse, and from the airport all the way by car to Selkirk, where we were to meet Nelson's chairman at his house. Our argument was on the point of whether the business was worth its valuation of assets or its valuation of earning power. When we stepped out of the car, and not until then, I told Gordon we would play it his way and base our offer on earnings.

In a remarkably short time we had bought the famous business – and in doing so on the basis Gordon had argued for, we had saved ourselves roughly £600,000.

'Now we will have a good dinner,' I said as we drove towards Edinburgh. 'Do you like spaghetti?'

I can imagine what he expected, but I took him to a café of my earlier acquaintance, and we had soup, spaghetti, and tinned fruit salad, for which Gordon now reminds me he paid the bill of 11s. 4d. It wasn't until I was just getting into bed, having arranged for an early call so that we could skip the hotel breakfast and catch the first flight to London, that I let my thoughts wander to stamp duty. On a purchase like this of Nelson's stamp duty would be sizeable. I couldn't get it out of my mind and for once wasn't able to sleep. When we met in the morning I told Gordon about it and when we got on the plane we were able to take only some coffee because we had the balance sheets and accounts spread out in front of us as we anxiously calculated the situation. By capitalizing some of the assets, we could reduce the stamp duty payable, we finally decided, from £30,000 to £20,000, I was satisfied.

I don't know exactly what Gordon thought of that trip, or what he thinks of it now, although he makes occasional oblique references to it, and how he was done out of a slap-up dinner and then his breakfast, but I think he learned a lot from it. About me, anyway. About how I am always open to be persuaded.

Thomson, like Winston Churchill, was an intuitive man with a strong personality, someone who thinks for himself and comes to some firm conclusions. Strength in this case means tenacity or perseverance. Such a person is not easily dislodged from an opinion, and perhaps never so from a conviction. He may not appear to be a good listener, but such leaders are persuadable. Paradoxically some 'good listeners', those who nod and smile at you and appear to be intent upon your words, are not in fact persuadable: they are acting a part.

The consequence is that if you wish to dislodge the Churchill or Thomson type of thinker you must be prepared to stand your ground and to argue. You may have to shout. Whatever your voice level your reasons must be extra-strong or compelling to move your leader from a partly dug-in position. But, because intuitive thinkers rely so much upon their depth minds, a reverse on the day does not necessarily spell defeat. Your arguments may appear to be trounced in the heated and noisy argument, but a few days later the penny may drop as the depth mind of the other person does its work.

Argumentative thinking in organisations is not the only, or necessarily the best, style. It has its drawbacks. The war of attrition between the trench lines of opinion can be very wearing on subordinates or colleagues. In the heat and dust of conflict things can be said which were better left unsaid. It calls for a high degree of trust and strong, persuasive subordinates.

On the other hand, argument gets the adrenalin flowing; it stimulates the mind in a way that the cool, detached reasoning advocated by management textbooks does not. It makes the subordinate or colleague work much harder at presenting his counsel on what should be done.

Between the poles of hot, noisy argument and an academic discourse there are many positions for you to choose from. Nor should you rigidly adhere to one point on that scale. In some instances you may want to contend and disagree based upon a firm (if ultimately moveable) point of view; in others you may want to generate an atmosphere of discussion rather than argument, where each possibility is considered by presenting the considerations for and against without prior commitment upon your part or anyone else's. It depends partly on the situation, partly on the matter under consideration, and partly upon your temperament.

Check your own thinking style

- Would you describe yourself as an argumentative thinker, one who likes to reason with others in a way that proceeds by argument?
- Or is your normal style more like that of the discussion leader, preferring a situation where neither party has already taken up a fixed position?
- Can you adapt your own approach in a flexible way to the style of others?

Whatever approach you adopt – or have thrust upon you – you should constantly remember the ends of argument. It is not to win or to avoid losing (that is another drawback of the conflict model of reasoning; it encourages this competitive mentality which often goes with being a high achiever).

The ends of argument are the truth, or at least greater clarity about the issue at stake or the true alternatives. The very word comes from the Latin *arguere*, to make clear. It should be essentially a rational process, a sifting of the consequences of a proposed course of action, or of several courses of action, so that the balance sheet of arguments for and against can be plainly read by the experienced and unprejudiced eye.

What is impermissible is that there should be no discussion, debate or argument in organisational life. For there will always be matters about which reasonable men and women may reasonably disagree. It is the ends and quality of the debate, more than the personal styles of those involved, which matters most.

Argument of the best quality is usually conducted by rational men who wish to become clear about what they should or do believe. They may be partly clear but not wholly so, or they may not be completely convinced. They wish to hear other points of view. They are in principle willing to change and accept those other points of view if they are more coherent and supported by the weight of evidence. They will entertain any opinion or adopt any of the proposed courses of action providing that reason – the balance of consequences judged in the light of the common purpose – emerges from the argument to favour it.

We owe this concept of argument to the Greeks. Thucydides

put into the mouth of the most famous Athenian statesman Pericles these words:

> 'The great impediment of action is in our opinion not discussion but the want of that knowledge which is gained by discussion prior to action. For we have a peculiar power of thinking before we act too, whereas other men are courageous from ignorance but hesitate upon reflection'.

John Milton stood in that tradition of Athens in its golden age, gave eloquent expression to argument as the God-given method by which rational men reached a consensus about the truth. In a pamphlet written during the English Civil War protesting against Parliament's imposition of censorship, he wrote:

> 'Where there is much to learn, there of necessity will be much arguing, much writing, many opinions; for opinion in good men is but knowledge in the making . . . Give me the liberty to know, to utter and to argue freely according to conscience, above all liberties'.

Milton, of course, was convinced that truth existed objectively and that we tend to doubt the strength of the truth to prevail. 'Let her and Falsehood grapple; who ever knew Truth put to the worse in a free and open encounter?'.

How to get it wrong

Rational argument, a 'free and open encounter', implies some rules, some common acceptance of criteria and a common commitment to truth. These will reduce the possibilities of errors, fallacies or deliberate cheating. If you encourage the winning-at-all-costs mentality, incidentally, you must expect more deliberate foul play. Tricks and cheating involve such motives, but you should also be on the alert for slipshod thinking as well. The following list of professional fouls, fallacies, slipshod thinking and pitfalls into which the unwary step, is far from exhaustive. But it gives you some idea what to look for.

(1) *Playing the man, not the ball*

Argumentum ad hominem, as the Roman rhetoricians called it, is argument calculated to appeal to the individual addressed more than to impartial reason. One dishonest version of it is to deliberately anger or frighten him so that emotion will cloud his thinking processes. You may see boxers trying to 'psych' each other in this way before a contest. A deliberately offensive or insolent manner, or making fun of matters upon which he obviously feels deeply, can serve to unbalance the other person. Knowledge of the trick makes the remedy obvious. However annoying the other person, you will best persuade him by keeping your temper under control.

There are plenty of other more subtle variations of arguing by concentrating on the human emotions and human frailties of your opponent:

- *Argumentum ad crumenam* – an argument to the purse i.e. one touching the hearer's pocket
- *Argumentum ad ignorantiam* – an argument to ignorance, i.e. one depending for its effect on the hearer's not knowing something essential
- *Argumentum ad invidiam* – an argument to envy or prejudice, i.e. appealing to those particular emotions

Almost any appeals to emotion, such as using words with an emotional bias – 'bloody obstinate' rather than stubborn or firm – come under this heading.

(2) *Argument by analogy*

This need not be a dishonest trick, more a potential pitfall. Analogy in the form of metaphor or simile is useful for the purposes of understanding an unfamiliar topic (see next chapter) and as a guide to further investigation. But its reliability must be constantly tested. For example, it may be used to *suggest* a conclusion, but it is incapable of *establishing* any conclusion.

Inference is based on the presumption that things whose likeness in certain respects is known will be found to be alike also in respects about which knowledge is limited to *one* of them. The conclusion that a product, because its development in some respects resembles that of a person, must by lapse of time grow feeble and die, is analogical.

Analogy rests on similarities, then, between related or apparently unrelated phenomena. But looking at those points of similarity can blind you to the divergences or differences. If pressed too far, analogy always breaks down. Therefore the best way to deal with it is by examining the alleged analogy in detail and pointing out where and why it breaks down.

Variations on the theme of arguing by analogy include *everyone is in the same boat* and *everyone is doing it*. Both imply analogies with other nations, societies, organisations or generalised individuals. The argument for pilfering, for example, tends to be that everyone is pilfering.

These analogies always break down if examined in detail. Some other nations may be in the same boat, say over unemployment, for the same broad reasons but under the microscope the ways in which their boat is different, or their management is different, or the national characteristics and situation is different, is conveniently left out.

The argument that everyone is doing it is usually a demonstrably false assumption. Moreover, numbers do not count in moral arguments. Therefore social surveys are of little value here. Arguments of this kind, anyway, usually fall under the heading of excuses rather than proper reasons.

(3) *Rationalising*

Excuses or reasons? That question leads us to rationalising, the giving of respectable reasons for actions. Hypocrisy, it has been said, is a tribute which vice pays to virtue. On the same principle, rationalisation is the tribute which our irrational selves pay to reason.

129

Rationalising can be a legitimate activity. You may have made a decision on intuitive grounds, and then seek to make it conform to rational principles.

In the perjorative sense, to rationalise means to attribute something, for example one's own actions, to rational and creditable motives without analysis of true (especially subconscious) motives. Giving excuses is an instance of the principle, because excuses are plausible but untrue reasons for conduct.

It is obviously very difficult when you are dealing with yourself, let alone other people, to discern between *reasons* and *rationalisations*. One strategy to adopt is not to give reasons where reasons are not called for. You do not have to justify loving someone, for instance, by giving reasons. The heart has its reasons as well as the head. 'When we ask for reasons when we should not, we rationalise'.

John Henry Newman, who said that, also added a significant thought for managers to consider: 'All men have a reason, but not all men can give a reason'. In argument the clever, articulate person always has an advantage. But a wise person will sense when he is talking to someone who has a reason which he has difficulty in putting into words.

Usually negotiation of any kind is accompanied by an exchange of reasons mixed with rationalisations. Experienced managers, like judges in law courts, can sort out the reason-making from the reason-giving. Providing, of course, they are not partisans themselves.

A particularly difficult form of rationalisation to detect is projection. People tend to impute (or project) their own motives or attitudes to others. A cynical or egotistical person, for example, often projects or imputes his own attitudes and motives to others. Even if you suspect projection, and point it out, arguments derived from amateur psychological analysis of the other person are unlikely to convince him. It is a useful discipline not to voice them: work on the assumption that he is as rational as you are!

Perhaps the most harmful type of rationalising is *buck-passing*, or projecting the blame onto someone else. This is what the bad carpenter is doing when he blames his tools. In its extreme form it involves making *scapegoats* of some person or group. Ineffective managers tend to see their superiors, colleagues or subordinates as lacking in competence, never themselves. A common form of defence for the manager who wants to hide a deficiency in a business meeting is to call into doubt the accuracy of the figures being examined. Unless the data are obviously correct, the mere act of casting doubt deflects criticism.

(4) *Drawing irrelevant conclusions*

The logicians call this one *ignoratio elenchi*, the ignoring of the argument or the matter at issue. You will see it done frequently in television interviews. The fallacy consists of disproving or proving something different from what is strictly in question. If the question is whether we should try to sell our goods in China and you prove conclusively that we have failed to sell them in Japan, you are guilty of this fallacy. It is like saying 'A must be true because of B', when in fact A doesn't follow from B at all. This is an example of a *non sequitur*, something which does not follow. A *non sequitur* always assumes an unproved cause. Thus, to say that we shall have riots this summer because youth unemployment is high is a *non sequitur* because it assumes rather than proves the cause. The fallacy of confusing consequence with sequence – because something happens after it, therefore it was caused by it – is a variation of the *non sequitur*.

Diversions, red herrings and non sequiturs come in many other shapes and sizes. You should aim to become quick to detect them. Try to see when someone is consciously or subconsciously attempting to shunt the whole discussion down a line leading to a side issue. Watch out for the assumption that once one has defeated an opponent on a trivial point one has somehow won the day on the main matter in contention. Deal firmly with irrelevant objections, especially on points of detail, and long diversionary exercises in humour.

The remedy for all irrelevance and diversion is to state again the real question at stake. The *non sequitur* and the *post hoc, ergo propter hoc*, 'after it, therefore due to it' assumption need to be pointed out for what they are – assumptions.

(5) *Reduction to absurdity*

The method of *reductio ad absurdum* is an attempt to disprove a thesis or proposed course of action by producing something that is both obviously deducible from it and obviously contrary to common sense. Equally it can be used to prove a proposition by showing that its contrary involves a consequence similarly absurd. Thus *reductio ad absurdum* is a tactic in the vitally important game of reasoning about consequences.

If you argued, for example, that the less labour you employ the less cost you incur, therefore to be completely cost-effective you should employ no labour at all, you are offering a *reductio ad absurdum* for the rest of the board of directors to consider. Carrying an argument to its logical conclusion nearly always produces a nonsense.

Euclid often used this method, incidentally, as a form of proof by assuming the contrary of the thing to be proved, and then showing that it led to an obvious absurdity.

(6) *The no decision/no action argument*

'There is much to be said on both sides, so no decision can be made either way'. The more intelligent you are, the more you are likely to tumble into the pitfall of the no decision/no action argument.

As an exasperated politician once declared in the British Parliament, 'someone should remind the Prime Minister that it is axiomatic that "the time is never quite right"; the atmosphere is always cloudy: the issue can never be sufficiently precisely defined and so it is never politic to proceed'.

Much the same kind of argument is advanced in boardrooms or in management meetings. Have you ever heard these 'arguments'

- Leave it until we are not so busy
- We're not quite ready for that yet
- Let's hold it in abeyance
- Let's give it more thought
- Let's form a committee

132

- It needs more work on it
- Let's make a survey first
- A working party should look into the whole area

These responses may be genuine. 'Leave undone whatever you hesitate to do', as an Eastern sage put it, is sometimes very good advice. But these phrases may be symptoms of a manager's deep reluctance to many *any* decision in the face of two or more equally balanced options at a time where a decision is clearly called for.

We cannot escape the necessity for action, and the growing realisation that there is much to be said on all sides does not absolve us from the need to judge where the balance of truth or wisdom lies, and then to act on that judgement. We have to choose the course of action which *on the whole* seems to be the best.

Closely related to the no decision/no action argument is another stock line 'Let us not do anything about X (which admittedly needs attention), because there is another problem Y which merits our attention as well'. This argument can be used in skilled hands against doing almost anything! Because we can do nothing about starvation in central Asia, for example, let us not bother to tackle poverty in Glasgow. This dishonest argument reflects a restrictive 'either–or' type of thinking. If X and Y are both evil then both should be dealt with. Likewise if both X and Y are good, then both should be encouraged.

The remedy for the no decision/no action argument is first to see clearly that making no decision is indeed a clear and valid option in a variety of situations.

Faced with mutually exclusive alternatives, then, you have a three-way choice:

1 alternative A
2 alternative B
3 opt out

If opting out is clearly an inadequate response, then you must resolve your dilemma by choosing A or B. If the choices are nearly equal it does not really matter which, *as long as it is one of them.*

Many people discover that in such situations it is useful to flip a coin to decide. There have been reports that having flipped a coin which determines the choice, they suddenly realise that that really is not the one they want and are thus able to select the other. As mentioned elsewhere, this is the depth mind doing its work, but late on cue. The no decision/no action argument is valid only when no action is really the best option.

(7) *All and some*

Although arguments in the cast of formal syllogisms, with accompanying statements like 'I am being logical now', are rare in boardrooms, there are plenty of fallacious arguments put forward in the name of reason. Many of them hinge on the use of *generalisations* followed by *deductions*.

Of course some generalisations are true, and we can deduct from them. 'All men are born' is true, therefore it is equally true that if he is a man he must have been born. But most such generalisations are suspect. 'All blue collar workers are idle' is as untrue as 'all managers are only out for the maximum possible profit'.

It is an aid to clear thinking if you insert the phrases 'tend to be' or 'have a tendency towards', if only to cover yourself. You can get away with saying that 'women tend to be intuitive', but not with 'all women are intuitive'. It is often a cause of unpopularity these days to be moderate and shun the media-catching exaggeration. But it pays off in the clarity of your thought. Caution over generalisations is not merely academic nicety. Too often decisions are based upon unwarranted statements or assumptions about what is generally the case.

Thinking revolves around the poles of the general and the particular, and getting the relationship between them as correct as possible.

Proof by selected instances is a variation of the all-and-some fallacy. Much dishonest argument consists of selecting instances favourable to our view while conveniently ignoring other instances which are either unfavourable or downright hostile to it.

One variation of the 'all and some' argument, which causes endless domestic and professional trouble, is generalising from selected instances *ad hominem*. Instead of saying accurately 'You have been late three times', you say 'You are *always* late'. Exaggerations intended for emphasis, signalled by such words as always and never, rob you of truth and the psychological advantages that go with it.

Arguments using statistics are notoriously liable to 'all and some' errors. For it is often unclear whether or not generalisations can properly be drawn from the samples. If 3,986 people in Boston now prefer bran products to cornflakes for breakfast, can we infer that *all* Americans do? Perhaps there is more experience of cereal choice in Los Angeles.

Statistics can be biased in the first place. Cooking or laundering the figures is not unknown. But more often than not it is the interpretation of the figures that is biased. In order to get the best out of this important source of data you need to be able to distinguish clearly between a *fact* and an *opinion* when these are cooked together and served up on your committee room table.

(8) *Middle-of-the-road arguments*

The assumption that the truth lies always in the mean position between two extremes is obvious nonsense. For every view can be presented as a mean between two extremes.

A second reason for distrusting this kind of argument is the fact that when you have two extreme positions and a middle one between them, the truth is just as likely to be at one end of the spectrum as in the middle. If I wanted to persuade you that two and two make five, I might point out to you that five is the safe position between the extremists who argue on the one hand that two and two make four and the other extremists who assert that two and two make six.

It is not to be supposed, of course, that the advocacy of a position or course on the grounds that it is a mean between two extremes is necessarily being dishonest. But it is suspect if that is your only reason for arguing its acceptance.

Another related fallacy is to use the fact of continuity between two poles or extremes to throw in doubt a real difference between them. To take a trivial example, if a man is growing a beard it is not easy to say precisely when he has a beard or when he does not, but you should not imply that there is no difference between a man with a beard and one without one.

The obverse side is the common mistake in reasoning of demanding or making a sharp distinction between those with beards and those without. These are the *black* or *white* thinkers: they cannot perceive all the intermediary shades of *grey* which lie between them. We create a barrier to clear thinking if we try to mark off a characteristic that is not capable of being so sharply defined.

Understand 'the law of the excluded middle'. See if this is a truly either/or situation, with no middle term. If so, you are in a true dilemma. But it may be one where there are a range of possibilities between the extremes.

> Here is an example of clear thinking by Edward Whymper. After seven vain attempts he was the first to reach the summit of the Matterhorn in July 1865. 'The line which separates the difficult from the dangerous is sometimes very shadowy, but it is not an imaginary line. It is a true line without breadth. It is often easy to pass, and very hard to see. It is sometimes passed unconsciously, and the consciousness that it has been passed is felt too late. If the doubtful line is crossed consciously, deliberately, one passes from doing that which is justifiable to that which is unjustifiable'.

The erroneous assumption that truth always lies in the middle of two extreme points must not be confused with true moderation. It is, of course, equally erroneous that those who take up the more extreme positions are being more 'radical' or 'honest' than their neighbours. Extremism of this kind is a strategy that pays only short-term dividends. It can be exceptionally disruptive in a negative or non-creative way. Leaders therefore tend not to be extremists. 'Moderation is a disposing, arranging, conciliatory, cementing virtue, said Edmund Burke. 'Moderation is the virtue only of superior minds'.

Conclusion

These suspect lines of arguments are merely examples. I have not written about the suggestive techniques of the salesman out to persuade a customer, because they are now familiar to all of us via television screens: the confident manner, the appeal to prestige, the air of authority, appeals to an undefined source, such as 'research shows . . .' or 'experts agree', the use of pseudo-technical jargon, the uttering of some preliminary acceptable statements before the doubtful proposition, the invoking of our thought-habits, prejudices and emotions. All are evidence of the power of suggestion, the attempt to slip ideas below our guard into the safe lodging of our depth minds, where they will erupt next time we are in the supermarket. Beware of the hidden persuaders! The price of truth, like freedom, is eternal vigilance.

But bad arguments should not blind us to the merit of having great and good argument as a preliminary to decision. The right-or-wrong, black-or-white kind of thinking should give way to a serious (but not necessarily solemn) argument about what it is reasonable or unreasonable to do in these circumstances. In many cases, it is better – if faced with a choice – to stir up a question without deciding it, than to decide it without stirring it up.

12 Useful originality

New ideas are essential for industry. New products and new ways of doing things are the lifeblood of successful enterprise. The theme of this chapter is creative and innovative thinking, the means by which ideas are born and nurtured. Such ideas do not result from following clearly prescribed steps but they can be encouraged. In order to stimulate the synthesising and holistic powers of mind you have to create the right conditions and apply certain principles.

What is creativity?

We all have new ideas. We vary, however, in the *quantity* we produce in our lifetime and still more in the *quality* of those ideas. Those people who have many new ideas with a high rate of excellent ones among them are called creative thinkers.

The word 'creative' should be bestowed rarely. It always

implies a value judgement. Therefore we should separate in theory the two dimensions of creativity: quantity and quality. There are prolific novelists in most countries but you can probably think of a writer who produced only a few works of real genius. You can place most creative thinkers on a scale in terms of a ratio of quality to quantity. (See Fig. 12.1)

An example of an A-type thinker is Dr R. Buckminster Fuller, the inventor, engineer, architect-designer and philosopher who died in 1983. After being expelled from Harvard and failing as a businessman he turned to architecture and invention. One of the most controversial architectural figures of our time, he produced designs for unprecedented types of structure which reflected his belief and optimism in the benefits of modern technology. Thus his Dymaxion House of 1927 saw the modern home not in terms of a walled structure but of technology servicing the human life within it. The house hung from a mast on a wire construction. The Dymaxion three wheeled car of 1932 similarly rejected the traditional coach maker's craft to produce a futuristic design.

But none of Fuller's inventions caught on before he conceived the Geodesic Dome, a linking of triangles into a strong and lightweight sphere, in 1949. It was another result of his

	QUALITY OF IDEAS	
High **A** High productivity and few quality ideas		**C** Many quality ideas in high quantity
B Not very productive and not producing many 'pearls'		**D** Many quality ideas with low productivity

PRODUCTIVITY OF IDEAS (High / Low)

QUALITY OF IDEAS (Low / High)

Figure 12.1   Creativity ratios

relentless pursuit of architectural forms along the path of mathematical logic. Architects hailed it as a genuine advance and Fuller's public image as a lovable crackpot began to change. Unlike classic domes, Fuller's did not depend on heavy vaults or flying buttresses for support. The weight load is transmitted throughout the structure, producing a high strength-to-weight ratio. More than 2,000,000 domes have been built, ranging from the US Air Force's early warning system establishments in Antarctica to the United States Pavilion at Expo 67 in Montreal. The Soviets were so impressed by the large dome at the 1959 US Exhibition that they bought it.

What determines 'quality' in creative thinking? There are many definitions, but common to all is a social judgement of value, often in terms of the three great value families: goodness, truth and beauty. Here we are concerned primarily with the first – goodness. Useful originality is a branch of it. A good idea is one that a critical mass of people deem to be both useful and original.

There are two approaches to defining the creative person, which correspond to the inductive and deductive methods of reasoning. You can study lots of such individuals and attempt to generalise, or you can work downwards and draw deductions from the general principles in this book. These are not alternatives; some combination of the two will yield the best results.

Either way it is a difficult exercise because creativity is not a separable ability. It cannot be discovered by a process of analysis. It is a holistic combination of mental abilities and

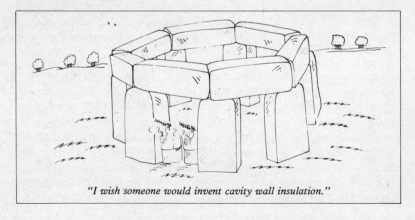

"I wish someone would invent cavity wall insulation."

qualities of personality, temperament and character. At the heart of that combination, however, is synthesising: the ability to combine together miscellaneous things into new wholes.

Necessity is the mother of invention

We can learn much from studying the qualities of creative thinkers. It is especially instructive to see how they scan their environments, feeling its needs deeply. New ideas are shaped, often using the depth mind principle, in response to a pressing need or an inconvenience.

Frank Hornby: a case study

Necessity certainly triggered off creative thinking in the mind of a butcher's clerk in Liverpool called Frank Hornby, who was born in 1863. He read Samuel Smiles' book *Self-Help* and took to making models for his children. The big breakthrough – combining self-help, engineering, models and children – came in 1900.

'One snowy Christmas Eve I was taking a long railway journey', wrote Hornby 15 years later, 'and as I sat in my corner seat my mind was, as usual, turning over new schemes for my boys' enjoyment'. His immediate problem was a shortage of parts for a model crane he had begun to construct. And then, Eureka! Hornby had it! He would make the same kind of part, perforated with bolt holes, so that they could be bolted in different positions and at different angles. 'I tell you, boys, that I was pleased when I hit upon this solution to our trouble, but I had no idea then that the few hours' close thought which I have given to my hobby were destined to change the entire future course of my life and work'.

Hornby called his invention Mechanics-Made-Easy and patented it in 1901. It was a simple idea – half-inch wide metal strips with bolt-holes a half-inch apart – but immediately successful. In 1907 he coined the name Meccano. By the outbreak of the First World War Hornby had made a million and was earnestly outlining his philosophy in a small book entitled *Frank Hornby: the Boy who made a Million with a Toy*. Samuel Smiles had not been forgotten: 'The Boy Scouts' idea is to do a helpful deed every day. Meccano is built on the principle of helpfulness. It gives every boy the opportunity to learn (while he is playing) how to do things that will help him to be successful when he becomes a man'. Indeed the invention had many industrial applications; it was indeed more than a toy.

During the 'twenties and 'thirties Hornby's products invaded nearly every middle-class home in Europe. Meccano sets grew larger and their models infinitely more complex. Meccano begat Hornby trains. Hornby trains begat Dinky toys. Meccano Magazine, founded in 1916, grew to 130,000 copies a month. There were editions in German and French; the Meccano Instruction Manual even ran to Russian and Cantonese.

The need to make educational toys for his own children was a sufficient spur or stimulus for Frank Hornby's depth mind to produce a creative synthesis of ideas and techniques. Sometimes an idea has to wait for a big enough need. The first zip fastener was demonstrated at the Chicago World's Fair of 1893, but had a number of defects, not least that it came apart easily. An improved version was tried out under the name C-Curity, but the zip did not catch on until the First World War, when the American armed services created a large market.

Many inventions come about as a response to personal inconvenience. The carpet sweeper was put together in 1876 by Melville Bissell, a china-shop owner of Michigan, because he suffered from headaches brought on by the dusty straw used for packing his wares. The first ballpoint pen was devised in 1938 by a Hungarian journalist, Laszlo Biro, because he got bored with blotting his work.

Britain can lay claim to one invention that revolutionized daily life. The world's first cannery was established in 1812 in Bermondsey, London. In those days canning was the job for expert craftsmen, the contents being introduced through a hole in the top and sealed with a soldered disc. But there was one snag. Directions on the label read: 'Cut around the top near to the outer edge with a chisel and hammer...' There could be no better demonstration of the maxim 'Necessity is the mother of invention'. The tin-opener had to be invented.

A modern millionaire who owes his fortune to a bright idea is Ron Hickman. 'Whenever anything irritates me, I try to think of better ways of doing it', he said.

The irritation that triggered the making of a fortune happened when he was fitting wardrobes at his home in Essex. He sawed into a new chair which he was using as a makeshift workbench.

That started him thinking about what a workbench should be like. Eventually he conceived the idea for a strong and ingenious workshop so compact that it folds to the size of a suitcase and can be carried easily from job to job. Called the Workmate, it won a Design Council Award and is today an international seller. 'Finding a really practical solution to everyday problems can be tricky', added Hickman. Even though lots of people have bright ideas, they don't test them hard enough. Often your first idea isn't right at all. This is where you need not just persistence but also ruthlessness to discard bad ideas. Unfortunately a lot of people don't have that'.

Hickman's words recall Edison on the subject of genius. Constantly taxed with being a genius, he gave some thought to the subject, coming up with the famous definition: 'Genius is one per cent inspiration and 99 per cent perspiration'. He enlarged on this to his secretary: 'Well, about 99 per cent of it is a knowledge of the things that will not work. The other one per cent may be genius, but the only way that I know to accomplish anything is everlastingly to keep working with patient observation'.

Even with his phenomenal workrate, however, it is unlikely that most of us would come up with even one invention of the calibre of the light-bulb in the course of a lifetime. And he invented not only the light-bulb but the phonograph, the telephone (concurrently in competition with Bell), the means of distributing electrical power, X-ray plates, and so on and on until the very end of his life. The capacity of the man is almost unimaginable. He was able to conceive of machines for recording what we hear, which turned out to be the phonograph; for recording what we see, which became the movie camera, which were outside the realm of anything existing then, so that their conceptualisation was a supreme work of imagination. Confronted with a problem, he was able to see how the solution might be arrived at. He could imagine, in the broadest terms, the short and long-term consequences of his inventions. And all that lay between him and these goals was a great deal of hard work, which he could not wait to dispose of as soon as possible.

Edison's life was ruled by the excitement of the hunt. He once said to a colleague: 'Beach, I don't think Nature would be so unkind as to withhold the secret of a good storage battery if a real earnest hunt for it is made. I'm going to hunt'. And hunt he did, whether for the secret of the battery, the right filament for the incandescent bulb, the best mixture for insulating cables, or

143

whatever the current problem might be, in the most methodical and exhaustive manner. There was never any time to spare; as soon as one problem was disposed of, another idea was waiting to be put to the test. There was never enough time – and he knew there was not – to investigate all his ideas. For example, it was not in the end Edison, but the Wright brothers, who made a successful aeroplane, although as early as 1889 he told a journalist: 'You can make up your mind . . . that these fellows who are fooling around with gasbags are wasting their time. The thing can't be done on those lines. You've got to have a machine heavier than air and then find something to lift it with. That's the trouble, though, to find the 'something'. I may find it one of these days'.

Widen your span of analogy

Lord Weinstock, in his early days as a television set manufacturer, made one of his most significant advances through reducing the cost of making a television set case by more than half. This arose because a bright production engineer, John Banner, knew a Scottish maker of church pews. The church pew man had found a way of creating certain veneers so that they could be cut up cleanly in curved shapes. Banner saw that by using these methods television set cases could be made on a special machine which sliced them up at the end of the line like Swiss rolls.

Mary Quant remembered seeing, as a young girl during the war, a tap-dancer in black stockings, black shoes, short skirt and a black top, with short-cut hair, 'She was chic', recalled the fashion designer. Hat-dress-shoes formed a whole. The seed of the mini-skirt, one of the most successful fashion innovations, had its source in that vision. Mary Quant is clearly a holistic thinker. The image of the tap-dancer was widely separated in time and in context.

The concept of *width* seems central to me. Our spans of analogy – the gap in time and space that our minds can bridge – vary considerably. Creative thinking often begins with the perception of a relationship – a spark of meaning – between two apparently unrelated things or ideas. 'The most original person is he who adapts from the most sources'. I would amend that saying so that it reads '. . . from the *widest apart* sources'.

Creative thinking, then, is bringing together things which are widely separated in time and/or space. John Banner, in the example above, and a considerable mental gap to bridge between two apparently unconnected technologies, or rather between an old technology and new one.

A classic illustration of the same principle at work is the invention of the seed drill by Jethro Tull, 'the greatest individual improver that British agriculture had ever known'. He was a musician and lawyer and went into farming out of necessity. Before his time sowing was done by means of a wheeled vehicle which held the seed in a container; and as the wheels turned the seed ran down through metal tubes or hollowed coulters underneath. The front of each coulter made a small furrow in the soil and the seed ran into it. A bush-harrow drawn behind the drill restored the soil and covered the seed. Earlier machines had failed because they could not effectively control the flow of seed from container to soil. Tull, the musician, solved the problem by adapting the mechanism on the sounding board of an organ to the drill he was making. He controlled the flow of the grain by means of a brass cover and adjustable spring, copied from the tongue in the organ mechanism.

The French doctor Laennec conceived and invented the stethoscope. The idea came to him when he remembered a boyhood incident of signalling to his friends by tapping out messages on a hollow log.

For the inventor a rich source of analogy is nature itself. For nature has creative and holistic properties embedded in its processes. Natural analogies can help you to discover or apply relevant principles. Here is a quiz:

Inventions or developments

List specific inventions or developments which were (or might have been) suggested to creative thinkers by the following natural phenomena. (Turn to p. 173 for answers)

(1)	human arms	(6)	earthworms
(2)	cats	(7)	a flower
(3)	seagulls	(8)	the eye of a fly
(4)	a frozen salmon	(9)	conical shells
(5)	spiders	(10)	animal bone structures

145

Interest, observations, storage in memory and synthesis are therefore the key constituents of creative thinking. A wide span of analogy is essential.

The depth mind dimension

Synthesis of apparently unrelated things or ideas carried out at the conscious level is not the same as free-range, natural creative thinking. In the latter the process of synthesis takes place at a less than conscious level. The rudimentary idea itself may emerge from the depth mind, as it did in the case of Frank Hornby and Mary Quant. Authors and poets report as much. C. Day Lewis spoke thus:

> What seems to happen for a poet is that experience sinks down on to the seabed of the unconscious. And lying there for a length of time, it is changed: 'those are pearls that were his eyes'. And one day a fragment of this buried treasure floats to the surface. It comes to me, very often, in an enigmatic form – a form of words, a brief phrase, which is attended by a special feeling of anticipation, excitement. It comes, more often than not, quite unexpectedly, when the mind is in neutral, or thinking of something else. I recognise it as the seed of a poem. It is in fact both a seed and a signpost; for it contains within it the potency of the still unwritten poem, and it points the direction this poem should take. I meditate on this *donnée*, this riddling clue, seeking to pick out, from the many possible meanings it suggests, the right meaning – the one which should grow into the theme of the poem'.[1]

We have met a similar phenomenon, related to decision making, in the chapters on intuition and the depth mind. You can see the same principle at work, but with much more emphasis on a holistic or growing synthesis – idea conception followed by a period of gestation in the mind's womb.

The ability to put your mind into neutral is worth developing, for there is plenty of evidence to support the poet's contention that ideas come at unexpected, relaxed moments, when you are not pressurising your mind for results.

Whenever the American businessman J. Pierpont Morgan

had to make a decision and the key thought would not come to him, he would deliberately put the problem out of his mind by getting out a pack of cards and playing solitaire for an hour. During or after the game the right decision would occur to him. Morgan had developed a simple relaxation technique to unblock the powers of his depth mind.

Scores of people have made creative breakthroughs by programming their minds and letting the purposeful unconscious part of it work for them. When they have ceased straining for the answer, it arrives in a flash, out of the blue, or as a hunch, while they are relaxing by doing something with hands or body. Agatha Christie claimed most of her ideas came to her while washing the dishes. Many men have ideas while shaving, driving or gardening. A British Nobel prize winner, Dr Godfrey Hounsfield, made the crucial breakthrough which led to the development of the body scanner while indulging in his favourite hobby, rambling. 'I'm very keen on rambling', he said later. 'It's a time when things come to one, I find. The seeds of what happened came on a ramble'.

> Edward H. Land, the inventor of polaroid photography, also had his bright idea while walking: 'I recall a sunny vacation day in Santa Fe, New Mexico, he wrote, when my little daughter asked why she could not see at once the picture I had just taken of her. As I walked around that charming town I undertook the task of solving the puzzle she had set me. Within the hour, the camera, the film, and the physical chemistry became so clear to me that with a great sense of excitement I hurried over to the place where Donald Brown, our Patent Attorney (in Santa Fe by coincidence) was staying, to describe to him in great detail a dry camera which would give a picture immediately after exposure. In my mind it was so nearly complete and so real that I spent several hours describing it, after which it was perhaps more real to him than even the ultimate reality'.

Learning to relax and listen for the answer is a necessary condition for creative thinking. Times just before going to sleep or shortly after awaking, when the body is in a state of complete relaxation, are often as fruitful as those of physical activity.

On rare occasions ideas come disguised in imagery during the course of a dream. Over a century ago Elias How alighted on the idea that led to the modern sewing machine. For weeks he worked on the machine, but one thing foiled him: how to thread the needle and still have the top of the needle attached to the machine. One night, after he had worked all day making no headway he fell into an exhausted sleep. He began to dream that some cannibals captured him and ordered, 'You must perfect the sewing machine within twenty-four hours or be eaten'. The cannibals danced round him. Then he suddenly noticed that the spear held by the cannibal chief had a hole in the blade near the point. He woke up with a start. He had discovered the solution! Put the hole in the sewing machine needle at the bottom near the point instead of at the top as in the needles of his day.

New ideas, insights or hunches can spring from your depth mind if you learn to interpose periods of hard mental work with times when you are lying fallow. Just lying down to sleep or relaxing in any other way without priming your unconscious with the question and data analysed as thoroughly as possible, will not produce anything worthwhile. We can apply here the principle of Louis Pasteur: 'Fortune favours the prepared mind'. But learning to unwind and to listen to your depth mind – trusting it in a warm and positive way to do its distinctive work – will take you forwards on your journey towards becoming a more creative person. Then, of course, when the creative idea has arrived you will be propelled into a great deal of hard work at the conscious level – possibly over years – to lick it into shape and bring the product or service to the market place.

Idea banks

It is useful to have a special place to store ideas related to a particular subject. The idea bank can be a stiff covered book, a file, a shoe box or a desk drawer or a combination of these. Whenever you have a good idea, write it down and bank it. Then, when you get ready to start some serious 'imagineering' you will have several previous ideas to get you started.

For example a single sentence copied into his notebook from one of his daughter's school-books gave author James Clavell the first bright idea for his novel *Shogun*. It said: 'In 1600 an Englishman named Will Adams came to Japan and became a samurai'. Clavell had been researching a book about modern day Japan, but intrigued by those words in the school text, he changed tack and immersed himself in learning about feudal Japan. Four years and 2,183 sheets of manuscript later Clavell had produced the 803 page best seller.

Use your ideas bank as a tool for creative reflection and thinking. Creativeness, as we have seen, implies bringing together into an unprecedented dynamic relationship things considered unrelated by conventional thought. The questioning, curious mind – innocent of intellectual subdivisions and conventional categorisings, and taking everying interesting as grist to its mill – can cause us to bring together in a very fertile and stimulating way diverse images, concepts and ideas.

You will notice mysteriously creative constellations of elements on a couple of pages of your notebook, but the range of material they contain has the unlimited potential of a kaleidoscope of new combinations and associations. You keep it all in a state of readiness by often browsing through them: ponder, dipping into them, glancing at a few pages last thing at night or on a train journey.

It is a much more intimate and profound process than dipping into other people's books, since the intuitive faculties have a much fuller part to play (and a more economical one, since everyone knows how maddeningly elusive ideas or facts are when you want them). Moreover, the original act of writing down the idea or morsel of information will help to commit it to your creative depth mind.

Innovation

The artist or inventor, the outstanding creative thinker in any field, differs from other men in degree, not in kind. As C. Day Lewis said,

> The instinct to make something, to make something grow – a table, a baby, a gardening trellis or a scientific hypothesis – we know to be universal. However humble or exalted the thing made, however ephemeral or long-lived, it has come into being through the operation of the creative spirit. It is possible, and

149

right to take pride in something which is the work of many hands
– a controlled experiment, a ship, an aircraft.

Most change is incremental rather than discontinuous.
Innovation means not merely introducing novelties but making
of changes to something already established. An example of this
more modest kind of creative change was the adding of milk to
chocolate by Daniel Peter in 1867 to make milk chocolate.
Innovation is an act that strives to produce small improvements
on what is accepted today. It seeks newer and better solutions to
old and current problems, solutions tied to a practical objective
and geared to a measurable operational result. The development
of the digital clock is a good example.

The need for innovation is universal. All products, whether
goods or services, require constant renovation and improvement. For change is happening all around us, and it can
suddenly outflank whole technologies. Think of the changes
which the makers of timepieces and writing implements have
had to cope with since the inventions of the pocketwatch and
fountain pen. The insatiable appetite of the public for useful or
'added value' novelty helps to fuel that drive for innovation.

The universal need for innovation in industry and commerce,
coupled with the fact that quite small changes can save costs or
improve products, opens the door of creativity to all who care to
enter. The Japanese with their Quality Circles (an idea introduced into Japan from America after the Second World War)
have shown the way to involve people in thinking creatively
about products and processes. Today, for example, the 43,000
work people of Japan's Toyota Motor Company submit some
250,000 ideas annually, aimed at eliminating or simplifying
production processes, introducing automation, improving
product quality or lowering the costs of materials.

The same principles apply in innovation as in creative
thinking proper. Improvements may lie far afield in another
country, another technology or even another time in history.
For example, there seems to be no connection between the
method of supplying scattered American farmers in the mid-
West pioneered in the 1920s by Sears, the US mail order giant,
and the success today of Marks and Spencer, but that creative
link exists. For Sears served as a model for Marks and Spencer.

The American farmer had little time or opportunity to go shopping. So the farmer received a catalogue and was given the novel guarantee of 'your money back and no questions asked'. Providing the service meant also creating new human skills, for example, by organising suppliers to achieve new standards of efficiency. Sears further adapted itself in the 1920s to the vast new urban market by placing its stores on the outskirts of the cities. After Simon Marks visited America, and Sears, in 1924 he re-thought the object of his firm, which was to be nothing less than a social revolution; that is, providing upper-class goods of better than upper-class quality, but at prices which the working and lower middle classes could afford.

Innovation requires a certain amount of humility. We have to build upon other's contributions, and allow our own to be built upon by others in turn. As the great physicist, Lord Rutherford, said, 'Every man depends on the work of his predecessors. When you hear of a sudden unexpected discovery – a bolt from the blue as it were – you can always be sure that it has grown up by the influence of one man on another, and it is this mutual influence which makes the enormous possibility of scientific advance'.

Creativity is therefore a social activity. The creative person depends upon the work of predecessors and colleagues. A degree of unselfishness is necessary in all thinking of quality.

Management actions

What can you do as a manager to encourage innovation around yourself. Here are some practical steps:

- Set an example by thinking about your own job and making some improvements. Remember that *activity* is not the same as *action*. Ships are not the only things that collect barnacles. Scrape them off your keel. If you change yourself, you will trigger off change about you.
- Look at your work team with a new eye. Sort out the innovators from those who have gone brown at the edges. Encourage each individual to come up with a quota of ideas.

151

- Work out a fair system for rewarding both the creative individual and the creative group. Small cash prizes may help. A few years ago, British Rail, for example, gave a £100 award to a train driver who suggested that the shiny metallic buttons on dustcoats issued to drivers for crawling around engines could be replaced by cheaper rubber composition ones. The idea saved about £2000 a year.
- Set aside time now and then for meetings designed to think creatively about innovations. Submit to it a list of suggestions or problems submitted by individuals for discussion. Take action on suggestions that pass muster.
- Develop an atmosphere of trust and warmth, a supportive and constructive climate where individuals are encouraged to think for themselves.

Reference

1 Day Lewis, C., *The Creative Spirit, More Sermons from Great St. Mary's,* Hodder and Stoughton, 1971.

13 Developing your thinking skills

This chapter aims to inspire you to develop your thinking skills. If you can do that it will contribute both to the success of your career and also to your mental health and happiness. For mental fitness is as important as physical fitness. Intellectual activities, sports and games can help keep your mind in trim.

This book rests on the assumption that decision making is fundamental to management. The actual decisions managers take vary enormously. If you analysed them many would centre upon the proper use of resources – people, money, plant – to achieve the ends of the organisation. What those ends are at a given time, how you measure them, what your resources should be: these should be matters for hard managerial thought.

What is an effective decision?

Before you can become a more effective decision maker you must reflect about the nature of an effective decision. It is not

153

necessarily a perfect decision – if such a thing exists. But it should be the best decision you are capable of making in the circumstances. What do such words as *good, better* or *best* – value judgements all – mean in this context? They are evaluations based on the way the decision achieves the aim or objective you had in mind. Does the arrow hit the mark? Does the decision affect your purpose?

In many circumstances there is no one correct course of action: several paths lead to the top of the mountain. Here decision making contrasts sharply with mathematical problem solving; there is only one right answer to the problem 'What do 36 and 64 add up to?' No so in management. Consider these reflections by C.E. Meyer, chief executive of Trans World Airlines:

> In the airline business as in any other, there exists something more like a continuum of possible solutions that produce a favourable result.
>
> For example, one of our competitors consistently has costs well above the industry average, but offsets that disadvantage with much higher revenue yields per passenger-mile and a higher proportion of the seats on its flights occupied by paying customers.
>
> At the other end of the scale, another of our competitors has historically had revenue yields and payload factors well below the industry average – yet it has overcome those operating deficiencies with unit costs dramatically lower than the industry average.
>
> Both are among the most consistently profitable airlines in the business. Each has adapted successfully to its quite different route structure and market opportunity and produced a winning combination of numbers.
>
> However, neither adaption would be possible for my own airline to emulate to its advantage. We, too, must find our own answers that respond to a unique situation.
>
> In shaping them, however, based on our experience with the unexpected, we shall try to make certain that a core element of our planning is to provide a reserve against the unforeseen.[1]

There are several ways that competing businesses can get it right, Meyer is saying. But that does not absolve the management of an organisation from the hard intellectual effort of chosing a course that is best for them. For each organisation is unique. Moreover being effective in thinking seldom means copying successful competitors. It often entails going back to first principles, reflecting deeply upon the changing situation and coming out with products that creatively blend the old with the new.

Ultimately then the test of a decision is whether or not it actually produces the goods. If it does it is then effective in the sense that accomplishes the intention; it gives the desired result. The difficulty faced by managers is that by the time you are in a position to judge results it could be too late; you will have already made the wrong decision. Therefore you should know the characteristics which will make a decision *liable* to be effective before you make it. If you or your organisation are deviating from these established norms during the process itself, then a warning red light should start flashing urgently in the cockpit of your individual or the corporate mind.

Note well Meyer's last point. Because you cannot know the result of a decision fully before you take it you are exposed to a degree of uncertainty. You can foresee some consequences for certain, others with a degree of probability, and still others as possibilities. But there may be some which are hidden from you for one reason or other. You will have to live with them. Other contingencies may also spring upon you. They can turn a good decision into a dead letter overnight. The actions of a competitor, a national strike and unforeseeable change in world prices: all these can intervene disastrously between a decision and its desired result. An effective decision maker will therefore take the unexpected into account. He will form a contingency plan that will enable him to modify his decision and to succeed in the face of the unexpected and still achieve his objective.

The risks involved, the sheer complexity of information and the balance of arguments for and against each course of action can breed indecision, the worst disease of corporate management. Prevention is better than cure. It may help you to remain decisive if you remember that in the nature of things managers must decide and decide quickly if so required.

Business is sometimes like a battlefield in that there is often no obviously right decision, just competing alternatives and a pressure to decide. It is better to make a wrong decision if it gets things moving than to make no decision at all. You can steer a moving ship. The alternative is inertia. If a wrong decision is made it can be often corrected as soon as the mistake becomes apparent. That is the principle of trial-and-error, an invaluable strategy for those who do not know what to do next.

The fear of getting it wrong creates a climate in which anxiety, delay and indecision take root. Paradoxically, many books and courses on rational decision making, often replete with algebraic equations, can feed that fear of getting it wrong. You need confidence to make decisions. That means ridding yourself of fear of making mistakes. Of course you will make mistakes but that is better than doing nothing.

The business of life is to go forwards. 'I'd much rather people took decisions, even if some turn out wrong, than were too scared to take risks', said Graham Clark, managing director of Rank Xerox. Would you agree?

Fletcher L. Byron, President of Koppers, makes the same point even more forcefully: 'Make sure you generate a reasonable number of mistakes. I know that comes naturally to some people; but too many executives are so afraid of error that they rigidify their organisation with checks and counterchecks, discourage innovation, and in the end, so structure themselves that they will miss the kind of offbeat opportunity that can send a company skyrocketing. So take a look at your record, and if you can come to the end of a year and see that you haven't made any mistakes, then I say, brother, you just haven't tried everything you should have tried'.

No manager in his right senses actually intends to make mistakes. He needs a checklist to ensure that he remains in the flightpath of the effective decision. Here are some key questions for your own checklist:

- Have I defined the objective?
- Do I have sufficient information?
- What are the feasible options?
- Have I evaluated them correctly?
- Does this decision feel right now I have begun to implement it?

When you do make a mistake, turn your regrets into gold. Go

156

back to your checklist and try to identify precisely where you went wrong. Then you will be learning by experience. That in turn will programme your depth mind. Next time that red light will flash on sooner.

The goal of consensus

Management is not solely about getting the intellectual quality of a decision right, important though it is to do so. It is about getting results through people. Therefore the manager will need to include other people in the process of decision making. For a decision will be effective only if it is fully implemented. People are more likely to put their hearts into it if they have shared either explicitly or implicitly in the making of that decision.

People can participate in the early stages of the process, leaving the leader to take the final decision. They can for example contribute information or suggest a possible solution. How far a leader should go in sharing a decision with another person or a group depends upon some key factors; the kind of decision it is, the knowledge and experience of those concerned and such situational factors as the time available for consultation. As I have discussed them several times elsewhere, I shall not go further into them here.[2]

Taking these factors into account there will be circumstances, especially as you rise up the promotion ladder, when you will want consensus. Yet many managers are not clear what consensus means in this context. Here is a definition:

When the feasible courses of action have been debated thoroughly by the group and everyone is prepared to accept that in the circumstances one particular solution is the best way forward, even though it might not be *every* person's preferred solution.

The most important test is that everyone is prepared to *act* as though it was their preferred course of action.

Granted a common commitment among group members to the purpose and aims of the organisation – a shared set of values – and an absence of aggressive or arrogant egoism in individual group members, consensus is usually forthcoming if a leader seeks it with determination and skill.

What is an effective thinker?

Proper decision making by individuals, groups and organisations presupposes a high level of basic thinking skills. Let us recall the main elements of productive thinking. The skills of *analysing* are constantly at work, breaking down larger entities into their component parts, sifting information and abstracting from it conclusions. When you are developing courses of action you are *synthesising,* putting things together. When you are seeking new ideas or combinations it is best to restrain deliberately from being critical – to suspend judgement. For ideas, like newborn lambs need a warm and encouraging climate. At the constructive core of criticism and all other forms of judgement there lies *valuing,* the assessing of relative worth. Lastly, the mind operates on different levels. A holistic approach – aided by a period of unconscious gestation – may help to produce the right decision for you: the pattern will grow in your mind and break surface in clarity.

An effective thinker should know which kind of thinking is needed at a given time and be able to do it himself or participate in it. For example if you want to think up a name for a new product it may be best to brainstorm it. Other sorts of problems may require very sophisticated forms of analysis.

The effective thinker knows that decisiveness does not always mean quick decisions. He is committed to *think it through.* The success or failure of some industries often depends upon a small number of key decisions – perhaps only one or two a year – and if these are wrong or not as good as they might have been, no number of subsidiary decisions can fully correct the situation. These key decisions – such as whether to join forces with a foreign competitor or to take a major innovative step to match competition – are vital from the strategic viewpoint. They must be studied with a scientific objectivity, employing all the methods of analysis and projection used in a fully professional manner. The options and the data, the arguments for and against each option, should be debated in conceptual forums among managers in the senior level long before the issue comes to the boardroom for decision. This cannot be done properly if senior management spend nearly all their time dealing with day-to-day problems of a short-term nature. If they delegate properly they will have time for proper strategic thinking.

Decision making, in the shorter or longer term, does not exhaust the role of thinking in management. There remains problem solving in the narrow sense of sorting out systems-type problems, such as those posed by the technology employed. There is the much wider contribution of the intuitive and imaginative powers, the opportunity-seeking and opportunity-creating faculties. Without them the progress of your enterprise will grind to a halt. Do you encourage them enough?

No one person has all these intellectual gifts. By accident or design however they will be present in a really high quality top management team. We should learn the social skills which will allow us to combine forces effectively with thinkers of complementary talent in the same organisation or outside it. Thinking is teamwork.

What then is an effective thinker? He is skilled in analysing, synthesising and valuing. He knows when and how to use his depth mind. He is receptive to intuition. His imagination can be brought into play to find new ways forward in apparently baffling situations. On occasions creative solutions will come to him mainly as a result of careful preliminary work. He is open to new ideas, even those suggested by unlikely analogies: his span of relevance is wide. Lastly, he is humble enough to know that others will excel him in some thinking skills and in specialised knowledge, and so he is able to link his mind with others in the search for truth.

Making an inventory of your skills

Improvement is always a relative notion. At any given time a person starts from a certain baseline. His mental faculties are genetic endowments; education will have drawn them out and trained them. The relative importance of these two aspects – nature and nurture – in a person's mental history is much debated. Opinions change as researchers produce their findings. What is clear however is that both are significant. Natural aptitude has to be there, especially for the more specialised forms of thinking, such as music or mathematics. But education of quality is essential for the general development of each individual's mind.

The first principle of self-development is 'know thyself'. Establish your baseline. You now yourself better than anyone else. What is your record of achievement as a thinker? What did your school reports, other feedback from staff and examination performance, tell you about your interests, aptitudes and temperament? Since leaving school or university in what ways have you grown in one or more of the three related fields of applied thinking: decision making, problem solving and creative thinking? Again, what does the feedback of colleagues – formal or informal – tell you about your areas for improvement? I suggest you write this information down on one side of a sheet of paper now, being as specific as you can.

Now turn the sheet over and list what you consider to be your good and your bad habits as a thinker. For bad mental habits – such as slipshod reasoning, making false assumptions, jumping to conclusions or not listening properly – can be unconsciously picked up all too easily. Check this list with a colleague at work and with your spouse or best friend.

Learning on the job

How do you acquire good habits? In the same way you received your bad ones – from observing others. You may not work closely with the modern counterparts of Thomson or Sloan, but you can still learn a great deal from observing and reflecting upon the living case studies around you: the senior managers to whom you are responsible, your colleagues and your subordinates. Do not ignore the latter: they may have had the benefit of more education and professional training than yourself. Why not profit from it?

The case of the merchant banker

At the age of twenty-five Jim Slater, newly qualified as a chartered accountant, applied to work for a Danish business-man, aged about fifty-five, named Svend Dohm. He had built up a group of fourteen private companies, besides other substantial investments. Dohm told Slater at the interview that he wanted to employ someone who asked questions – a promising sign. They got on well together and Dohm appointed him to be chief accountant – and subsequently general manager of one of his companies called Renu. It was losing a lot of money. Having put that right Slater was given another ailing company in the group called National Colours to nurse back to health.

I was fortunate, as a young man of twenty-five, to be given such full responsibility for the complete reorganization and management of companies such as National Colours and Renu. At first I could hardly believe that I had the authority to change things so drastically. However, money was critically short in the group and the problems were very pressing so I soon found that I was taking action quickly because decisions had to be made or the businesses would have foundered. As I continued to take decisions, and began to see things happen as a result, my confidence grew.

I learned a lot from Dohm, who was an amazing character. He was the first man who really taught me 'contrary thinking'. This was the principle on which he made his many stock exchange investments. For example, immediately after the war he bought German bonds, when most people would not have believed in the possibility of Germany recovering to the extent it did, and made a fortune on them. He also used to invest in small, out-of-the-way companies that were not doing very well. His main interest was in underlying assets as opposed to immediate earnings and he would buy when things looked bad. He was one of the very few investors who applied contrary thinking.

Dohn had two other maxims, which impressed me at the time and which I have endeavoured to follow ever since. The first was expressed in a motto across his mantelpiece which said, 'It can be done'. Whenever a problem arose, he always sought a positive solution, insisting that it could be found; the possibility that there was no answer simply did not occur to him. This approach is one which I consider invaluable. Dohm's second maxim was, 'Always try to turn a disadvantage to an advantage'. If a customer wrote to him complaining about some service or other, he would reply in such a way that he would make the man a customer for life; if one of his factories had a fire, he would immediately ask how the plant and machinery could be reorganized when it was replaced, to make the lay-out better than it had been before. Dohm was a difficult man to beat.[3]

161

The good habits in thinking revolve like planets around the sun of truth. As a manager you can do not better than to emulate Lord Thomson, of whom a senior colleague wrote: 'his most memorable quality was his instinctive habit of telling the truth. His strength, which was very great, particularly in dark moments, made him enjoy truth when another man would have found illusion more comfortable. He always faced reality and he always believed that he could do good business in terms of the reality that he faced.'

These associated habits of seeking and speaking the truth have one incalculable benefit in human relations, one which far outweighs all the mental effort required to see reality, and the moral courage sometimes needed if you are going to respond to it with the appropriate action. Truth begets trust. Trust is the bedrock of partnership.

In order to learn about what for example original thinking or imaginative thinking or effective decision making means at work, we rely upon experience. You cannot learn those things at school from schoolmasters or at university from academics. Managers are your teachers if only by example. It may be your good fortune to work closely with a businessman of genius – providing that you observe him closely.

Alfred Sloan worked with William C. Durant, the founder of General Motors. He recalled that Durant 'would proceed on a course of action guided solely, as far as I could tell, by some intuitive flash of brilliance. He never felt obliged to make an engineering hunt for facts'. Sloan, perhaps the greatest manager of his day, concluded: 'The final act of business judgement is intuitive'.

May I emphasise the suggestion made in the last chapter that you should keep a stiff-covered notebook in which you enter your tentative conclusions, helpful examples, principles, new ideas, management proverbs and so on. Make notes from the books or articles you read which have a bearing upon the subject. Try to imagine what mental habits you would like to have developed at the end of three years: list them in your book. Go through your notebook carefully every month or so, looking backwards to see what else you have learnt. Think about thinking – it is your profession.

Keep mentally fit

Profession, work, occupation – these dominate our lives. But there will come the day when you will stop managing. Instead of retiring at sixty-five or sixty you may be doing so at fifty-five. Without the mental stimulus of decision making at work will your brain continue to be healthy? Most of our brains do not get enough exercise. They are like muscles which need to be used and stretched if they are to remain healthy. Exercises of a mental kind if done regularly, will help to keep your mind in trim.

We lose some of our brain cells every day. People who use their brains most, such as lawyers, professors and doctors, lose fewer cells daily than those who do not. Farm workers, bus drivers, shop assistants and white collar work people doing routine jobs in offices need to supplement their occupations with the vitamins of intellectual exercise if they wish to stay mentally active into old age.

The best way to maintain good blood circulation in your head, which prevents cell loss, is through using your brain. Thinking is an essential therapy. We should all develop our mental equivalents to daily exercises, walking briskly or jogging. Mental exercise, like physical exercise, should be as interesting and as much fun as possible: that way you are likely to persevere longer with it. Start with reading some demanding non-fiction books. Make notes; argue with the author; draw your own conclusions.

How to avoid stimulus deficiency

Few of us – perhaps none – are entirely self-motivating as thinkers. We need the outside stimulus that comes from other minds. Besides providing you with the stimulus to think for yourself other people can also give you new ideas. Again it is worth quoting Lord Thomson, for he capitalised on this fact, as every sensible manager should:

> I try to make friends wherever I go and it is my fond belief that I usually succeed. The way I look at it, everyone has an idea and

one in a dozen may be a good idea. If you have to talk to a dozen people to get one good idea, even just the glimmering of an idea, that isn't wasteful work. People are continually passing things on to me, because I have given them to believe that I will be interested, I might even pay for it! Sometimes, usually when it is least expected, something comes up that is touched with gold.

Seek new experiences. Ruts and routines are enemies of mental fitness: they induce staleness and rigidity. These will turn eventually into mental arthritis if you do nothing. A fresh challenge can bring life flooding back into the dry cells of your mental battery.

New experience is especially vital for the manager who has been in the same job for more than five years. Sometimes the job or its context changes so markedly that interest is renewed; sometimes it remains static and becomes boring. Sustained boredom, needless to say, is a killer of brain cells. Ask for promotion or a sideways move or to be sent on a course – anything to restore your freshness of vision, enthusiasm and appetite for work. If your pleas are ignored, explore the option of changing your job. There could be risks involved in pursuing that course of action. But there are also risks in allowing yourself to vegetate gently in a job which no longer provides you with any intellectual challenge. Avoid terminal mental lethargy.

Conclusion

How far you develop your abilities as a practical and productive thinker is largely up to you. Your starting point in terms of natural mental aptitudes and academic record is not as important now as your motivation to succeed as a manager.

If it has done nothing else I hope this book will have made you think – and think hard – about the core function of your trade as a manager: effective decision making. Above all, it should have made you want *to exert yourself* as a practical thinker.

You should deliberately stretch yourself to learn all you can about the art of making decisions. Even if you have few original ideas you should at least set yourself the goal of understanding more fully the creative process and how ordinary people can contribute to it. For the future of industry, indeed the future of our civilisation, depends upon the creative flair and innovative genius of people.

Decision making has to be learnt on the job, partly from wise practitioners in the craft and partly by personal experience. As experience accumulates you will be able to move with greater sureness and speed, although – as in all worthwhile fields of human life – there is always more to be learnt. We can always widen our interests, both for profit and pleasure. Work should be the chief outlet for your educated talents. But a sensible self-development programme, based upon a realistic estimate of your abilities, interests and temperament, will both enhance your contribution at work and enrich your whole life beyond it.

Therefore, in conclusion, you have your intellectual strengths and weaknesses. Now use that self-knowledge to develop your foundation upon which to build your mind, using the principles set out in this book. Re-read it at least twice. Do not expect too much and do not attempt too little. For encouragement when the going is hard remember the old proverb: 'God is with those who persevere'.

References

1 Wild, Ray, *How to Manage,* Pan, 1983.
2 Adair, John, *Effective Leadership,* Gower and Pan, 1983, and *Training for Decisions,* Gower, 1978.
3 Slater, Jim, *Return to Go: My Autobiography,* Weidenfeld and Nicolson, 1977.

Answers to problems

"Who Is Going to Barker Street?"

**The baker is Bob Barker. Bert's last name is Burke.
Bart Burger is going to Barker Street.**

Taxi Number:	1	2	3	4	5
First Name:	Brad	Bob	Bart	Brian	**Bert**
Last Name:	Bunger	Barker	Burger	Baker	Burke
Profession:	barber	**baker**	banker	butcher	broker
Wife's Name:	Betty	Beatrice	Barbara	Brenda	Bernice
Destination:	Baker St	Burton St	**Barker St**	Burbon St	Barton St

From clues 2, 4, 6, 7 and 11, we know: Barbara's husband gets into the third taxi, the last taxi goes to Barton Street, the butcher gets into the fourth taxi, Bob gets into the second taxi, and Mr Bunger gets into the first taxi. The remainder of the puzzle can be solved only by combining clues and eliminating possibilities.

You know that the butcher is in the fourth taxi, so Mr Burger

166

(Clue 16) must be in the third taxi. And since Mr Burger gets into the third taxi, Brenda must be the wife of the man in the fourth taxi (Clue 10).

The next step is to combine clues 5 and 9. Burton Street is the home of Beatrice Barker; therefore, the only place these clues will fit is under taxi number two.

Clue 12 is next. Mr Baker must get into the fourth taxi since it is the only place where a last name and destination are still not found.

Clue 14, logically, follows. Since the barber lives in Baker Street (Clue 13), and is three taxis in front of Brian (Clue 15), the only place the barber could be is in the first taxi. Therefore, Brian's last name is Baker.

Since Bernice is married to the broker (Clue 8), the only place for these two items of information, by elimination, is under taxi number five.

By elimination, taxi number three now accommodates Clue 3 (Bart is the banker).

The only place Clue 1 now fits is taxi number one.

What it takes for top jobs – the answers of 200 chief executives

Ranking of attributes most valuable at the top level of management	Attribute developed mainly by academic work	Attribute developed mainly by professional work
1 Ability to take decisions	1	9
2 Leadership	0	9
3 Integrity	1	6
4 Enthusiasm	1	6
5 Imagination	1	6
6 Willingness to work hard	3	3
7 Analytical ability	7	2
8 Understanding of others	0	9
9 Ability to spot opportunities	1	8
10 Ability to meet unpleasant situations	0	9
11 Ability to adapt quickly to change	1	9
12 Willingness to take risks	0	8
13 Enterprise	1	4
14 Capacity to speak lucidly	4	5
15 Astuteness	1	9
16 Ability to administer efficiently	1	9
17 Open-mindedness	2	6
18 Ability to 'stick it'	3	4
19 Willingness to work long hours	3	3
20 Ambition	2	5
21 Single-mindedness	3	5
22 Capacity for lucid writing	9	1
23 Curiosity	4	3
24 Skill with numbers	7	2
25 Capacity for abstract thought	7	2

Exercises in logical thinking

1   Either the first or the fourth statements must be true, because they cannot both be untrue. Therefore either Mr Carpenter or Mr Mason is the painter.

   Since the second and third statements must both be untrue, Mr Mason is the carpenter, Mr Carpenter the painter and Mr Painter the mason.

2   Each barber must have cut the other's hair. The logician picked the barber who had given his rival the better haircut.

3   The parrot was deaf.

4   Among the 97 per cent of the women, if half wear two earrings and half none, this is the same as if each wore one. Assuming that each of the 800 women is wearing one earring, there are 800 ear-rings.

5   The trains are travelling one at 60 mph and one at 40 mph towards each other. Between them they will cover 100 miles in one hour. Therefore they will meet after one hour. The plane is flying backwards and forwards at 80 mph until they meet. Therefore the plane is flying at 80 mph for one hour. With this reorganisation of relationships within the problem you should be able to work out the answer for yourself.

Think it out (2)

1   Carry cat to car and return empty-handed
2   Carry Sara to car and return with cat
3   Leave cat in house and carry Roger to car
4   Return empty handed and carry cat to car

Think it out (4)

(a)   How old is the Naval Captain? – 52
(b)   What is the nationality of the football player? – Dutch

Professions:	Engineer	Teacher	Journalist	Singer	Captain
Nationalities:	Dutch	Italian	English	German	French
Ages:	40	24	32	21	52
Sports:	Football	Swimming	Volleyball	Athlete	Handball
Destinations:	Birmingham	Manchester	London	Newcastle	Plymouth

This is one way of solving the problem:
Keep working through the facts from 1–14 in sequence.
Concentrate on clues for which there is only one answer.
That is:

1 The Engineer is seated on the extreme left.
2 The volleyball player is seated in the middle.
14 The Engineer is seated next to the Italian.

Then look for information which has only two possible answers. That is:

11 The passenger from France is seated next to the German.

If you place the Frenchman in the middle and the German on his right you are wrong. You can progress but will not be able to complete the whole problem.

If you place the German on the far right and the Frenchman next to him you are correct and you can progress logically, since you will find that other items of information now have only one answer. That is:

3 The Englishman is the journalist.
7 The handball player is French.
8 The passenger from Holland is bound for Birmingham.
13 The 24-year-old passenger is seated next to the passenger who is travelling to Birmingham.

Then look for other information which has only two possible answers. That is:

5 The teacher's sport is swimming.

If you place the teacher next to the engineer you are correct and can progress logically. If you place the teacher on the far right you are wrong and will be unable to solve the problem. It will be necessary to return to this point and take the other alternative.

If you have placed the teacher next to the engineer then progress logically to find other items of information that have only one answer.

10 The athlete is bound for Newcastle.
There is now a blank space in sports, so from the information at the beginning of problem:

The man from Holland must play football.

6 The naval captain is travelling to Plymouth.
4 The singer is 21.
9 The passenger bound for London is 32.
12 The 40-year-old passenger is seated next to the passenger who is bound for Manchester.

The Captain is therefore 52.

The Missing missile

This problem, used for selecting potential army officers, was published in the British press during 1973 as part of an advertising campaign. A reporter, A.J. McIlroy, who had not undergone military training except at secondhand, so to speak, by reporting Army operations in Ulster and some other countries, submitted the following plan.

The McIlroy plan

I would commit my force to a landing in the west at Toe, taking the good southerly route overland to the search area to reach it, according to calculations on the figures provided in the test, at around 17.30 hours, well over an hour before the enemy submarine is expected even to reach the island (at sunset, 18.45 hours).

(The test says the boats could be rowed at only up to 2 mph. The easier southerly overland route could be crossed at 4 mph but the other possible routes at only 3 mph. The cliffs in the north east could be climbed at about 300ft per hour.)

My course of action would avoid the risk in an ill-equipped climbing party scaling the cliffs at Heel and the delays and exhaustion in rowing seven miles from the cargo boat in rough seas to Arch, the southerly landing point.

I dismissed alternative plans which involved dividing my force and attacking the enemy for three main reasons.

1 The submarine was aware it had been spotted, so there was

171

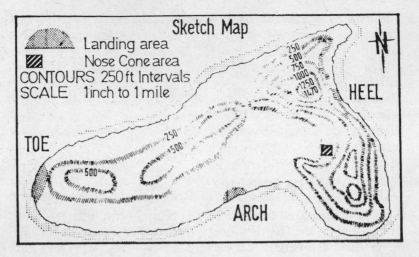

little prospect of surprising the landing party. There was no certainty which landing point the submarine would choose.

2 The submarine landing party would certainly be better armed and our 0·38 pistols and shotguns are more suited to defence than to attack.

3 An enemy able to redirect a rocket in this way would certainly have pinpointed the nose cone's position, making it imperative for my force to press home its time advantage, reach the search area and find the nose cone without delay.

The expert's view

Brigadier W.F.K. Thompson, Defence Correspondent of the *Daily Telegraph*, wrote: 'Our candidate has met the main purposes of the test which are to see whether a would-be officer is able to distinguish the essential factors in a situation and to muster them so as to arrive at a logical plan of action.

He appreciated that while time was on our side and that the enemy would only arrive off-shore as it was getting dark, he would, on the other hand, almost certainly be better armed. It is essential, therefore, that we should be first to reach the rocket head.

172

Since the enemy had the technical ability to divert the rocket, our candidate, quite rightly in my opinion, considered that they are likely to be as well aware of its exact location as we are.

Our candidate, I feel, has certainly qualified to undergo the further tests required by the Officer Selection Board. These include an ability to contribute to group discussions, to express views clearly, both verbally and in writing, and to give practical demonstrations of effective leadership in solving practical problems'.

An option problem

The flight engineer decided to work through the standard checklist yet again. Engines restarted when the aircraft was at 800 ft.

Inventions or developments

1   A young English designer named Carwardine approached the firm of Herbert Terry at the beginning of the 1930s with the proposal that they should build a desk light employing the constant-tension jointing principles found in the human arm. The company agreed, and the Anglepoise light was the result. From that time it has been in production, scarcely altered except for details and finishes.
2   Cats eyes in the road.
3   Spitfires.
4   Clarence Birdseye took a vacation in Canada and saw some salmon which had been naturally frozen in ice and then thawed. When they were cooked he noticed how fresh they tasted. He borrowed the idea and the mighty frozen food industry was born.
5   They could have suggested the principle of independent suspension.
6   The burrowing movement of earthworms has suggested a new method of mining which is now in commercial production.
7   In Edinburgh botanical gardens there is a plaque com-

memorating a flower which inspired the design of the Crystal Palace.

8   Sir Basil Spence, the architect of Coventry Cathedral, was flipping through the pages of a natural history magazine when he came across an enlargement of the eye of a fly, and that gave him the general lines for the vault.

9   Linear motors.

10 Ball-and-socket joints.

Index

Adrian, Lord 96
American Telephone and
  Telegraph Company 65
Analysing 29, 31, 32, 159
  analytical ability 23, 25, 31, 34
  asking yourself questions 36
  deduction 38–9, 44
  exercises in logical thinking 39–40
  filleting arguments 38–9
  identifying good analytical mind
    31–4
  induction 38, 39, 44
  logic of situation 43–4
  logicians' methods 36–8
  missing missile exercise 44–8
  organising facts 41–3
  returning to first principles 34, 35
  thinking backwards 41
Antietam, Battle of 107–8, 113
Archimedes 67

Archytas 67
Arguing 123–5
  all and some argument 134–5
  argument by analogy 128–9
  argumentum ad crumenam 128
  argumentum ad hominem 128, 135
  argumentum ad ignoriantiam 128
  argumentum ad invidiam 128
  buck-passing 130–1
  drawing irrelevant conclusions 131
  fallibility of statistics 135
  false arguments 127–37
  middle-of-the-road arguments
    135–6
  no decision/no action argument
    132–4
  projection 130
  proof by selected instances 134
  rational 126–7
  rationalising 129–31

reasons for 126
reductio ad absurdum 132
Awa, Kenzo 104

Ballpoint pen 142
Banner, John 144, 145
Bar Lev, General 95
Bell, Alexander Graham 143
Biro, Laszlo
invents ballpoint pen 142
Bissell, Melville
invents carpet sweeper 142
Body scanner 147
Bondi, Sir Herman 27
Bragg, Sir Lawrence 70
British Holistic Medical Association
52
British Leyland 64
British Rail 152
British Steel Corporation
decision making in 7–8
Burke, Edmund
on moderation 136
Burns, Tom 10
Burnside, Gen. Ambrose 107, 108,
113
Butlin, Billy
develops holiday camps 117
Byron, Fletcher L. 156

Carpet sweeper 142
Carroll, Lewis 24–5
example of deduction by 39
Central Intelligence Agency (CIA) 88
Chicago World's Fair, 1893 142
Christie, Agatha 147
Christies, London 83, 84
Churchill, Winston 88, 114, 124, 125
on imagination in battle 77
support for Dr R. V. Jones 88–90
Cicero
on probabilities 122
Clark, Graham 156
Clavell, James
Shogun 148–9

Comino, Dimitro 34
Conceptual thinking 58–60
and decision making 63–5
conflict between concrete and
abstract 58–9, 66–7
problem of defining 'concepts' 60–3
reflective thinking 65–7
Conscience 101
Consolidated Gold Fields 31
Creativity 138–41
creative imagination 116–17
depth mind dimension and 146–8
idea banks 148–9
innovation and 149–51
ratios 139
triggered by necessity 141–4
widening span of analogy 144–6
Criticism
negative 118
true 118–19
Cuba
Bay of Pigs invasion 88, 116

Dayan, Moshe 94
Decision making 165
and pay relativities 2
five point plan for 4–6, 13, 156
goal of consensus 157
illogical factors affecting 6–7
nature of effective decision 153–7
part played by depth mind 105–6
Depth mind 23–5, 100–1, 104–5
creative thinking and 146–8
memory 24, 25
part in decision making 105–6
preconscious 24
post-action operation of 101–2, 134
'sleeping on' a decision 25
subconscious 24, 25
unconscious 24, 105
Dexion Ltd 34
Dixon, Prof. Norman
on stress 12–13
DNA 33
Dohm, Svend 160, 161
Durant, William C. 162

Edison, Thomas 75
  defines genius 143
  inventions 143–4
Edwardes, Michael
  on discussing BL with PM 64–5
Einstein, Albert 27, 51, 75, 110
  on intuition 94
  relativity theory 85–6
Emotion 26–7
  and intuition 95–6
  hedonic response 26
Euclid 132
Eudoxus 67
Expo 67, Montreal
  US Pavilion 140

Finniston, Sir Monty 7, 8
Ford, Henry 31, 98
  intuitive approach 98
Ford, Henry II 99
Ford Motor Company 98
Freud, Sigmund 24
Fuller, Dr R. Buckminster 139
  Dymaxion car 139
  Dymaxion House 139
  Geodesic Dome 139–40

GEC 55
  problems at Stafford plant 17
General Motors 98, 123, 162
Gestalt school of psychology 51–2
Getty, Paul 97, 120
Grahame, Kenneth 69
  The Wind in the Willows 69
Greenwood, Ron 76
Grigg, P. J. 89

Hawtrey, Sir Ralph 88
Hay-MSL ManagementConsultants
  18, 59
Hegel 49
Heisenberg, Weiner 51
Herrigel, Eugen
  Zen in the Art of Archery 104

Hickman, Ron
  invents Workmate 142–3
Hilton, Conrad
  business intuition 102
Hitler, Adolf 96, 112, 113
Holistic thinking 49–50, 159
  about problems 53–4
  holism defined 50
  holistic approaches 51–2
  holistic vision 50–1
  importance of nature and growth
    to 54–5
  numeracy 55–6
  opposition to analysis 50, 51
  routes leading from 56–7
Hornby, Frank 146
  development of Meccano 141–2
  development from Meccano 142
  Frank Hornby: the Boy who made a
    Million with a Toy 141
Hounsfield, Dr Godfrey
  visualises body scanner while
    rambling 147
How, Elias
  invents sewing machine 147–8

Imaginative thinking 69–71
  brainstorming 71, 117
  development of 78–9
  fantasy 73
  imagination in perspective 80–1
  in action 76–8
  practice in using imagination 73,
    75, 76, 80
  range of 71
  relation to holistic thinking 69
  test of imagination 72
  thinking and imagination 73–8
  thinking in pictures 70–3
Intuition 92–4, 99, 159
  as symptom as anxiety 94, 95
  business flair 96–8
  in practice 94–5
  relation with emotion 95–6
  test of 93
  trusting to 94
  women's 92

Jones, Dr R. V. 88–90
  'bending the beam' 89

Kappel, Frederick R.
  on reflective and action thinking
    65–6
Kennedy, Pres. John F. 88, 116
Koppers Company 156

Laennec, Dr
  invents stethoscope 145
Land, Edward H.
  invents polaroid photography 147
La Vallete, Jean de 91
Leach, Bernard
  criminal copying of his pottery 77
Learning roadblocks 27
Leonardo da Vinci 75, 79
Lewis, C. Day
  on creative spirit 149–50
  on poetic creativity 146
Lincoln, Pres. Abraham 108

McLoughlin, Luke 8
Management 1
  attributes considered most valuable
    in 30
  balance between productivity and
    human values 15
  centrality of decision making 2–3
  concept of 62–3
  goal of consensus 157
Managers
  avoiding stimulus deficiency 163–4
  decision making checklist 4–6, 13,
    156
  failure to use skills of work force
    16–19
  generalist nature of abilities 87
  learning on job 160
  need to encourage innovation 151–2
  problems with people 13–14
  rational 3–4
  self-development 159–60
  stress and 13–14
  time division of activities 8–10

Marks and Spencer 150
Marks, Simon 151
Marks, Karl 49
Meir, Golda 97
  on ignoring one's intuition 94–5
Mental functions 20–1, 28
  analytical ability 23, 25 See also
    Analysing
  brain power 22, 28
  depth mind See separate entry
  managing emotion 26–7
  roadblocks to learning 27
  synthesising ability 23, 24, 49
    See also Holistic thinking
  valuing ability 23, 25 See also
    Valuing
Meyer, C. E.
  on airplane business planning 154,
    155
Milk chocolate 150
Mill, John Stuart 68
Milton, John
  on need for argument 127
Mintzberg, Henry
  characterises managerial activity
    10, 11
  reclassifies managerial role 10–11
Morgan, J. Pierpont
  decision making technique 146–7
Mozart, Wolfgang Amadeus
  on composing 69–70

Napoleon
  on crossing the Alps 113
Newman, John Henry 130
Nicholaidis, Nicholas
  on decision making 6–7

Options 107–9, 121–2
  assessing consequences 119, 121
  check-list 111–12
  developing range of 109–11
  do-nothing option 111
  false assumptions and 113–14, 121
  generating more 115–19

importance of probability 120–1, 122
limitations on choice 114–15
problem 112
process of elimination 110
risk 122
Organisations
contractual relations with employees 14–15
'managerial schizophrenia' 15–16
traditional distinction between managers and work people 16
Osborn, Alex 117

Pasteur, Louis 148
Pericles
on need for discussion before action 127
Peter, Daniel
invents milk chocolate 150
Plato 67
Plutarch
on Archytas and Eudoxus 67
Polaroid photography 147
Prince of Wales, HMS 114
Probability 120–1
Problems
types of x–xi
Pugh, Lionel 7–8

Quality Circles 150
Quant, Mary 146
devises mini-skirt 144

Rank Xerox 156
Repulse, HMS 114
Roosevelt, Pres. Franklin D. 27
Rusk, Dean 116
Russell, Bertrand 84
Rutherford, Lord 151

Sainsbury, John
on imagination in management 78

Sanger, Dr Frederick
analytical ability in biochemistry 33–4
Schiller, Johann 117
on intellect's restraint on creativity 118
Sears Company 150, 151
Sewing machine 147–8
Shakespeare, William 75, 92, 123
Singapore
falls to Japanese, 1942 114
seaward fortifications, 1930s 113
Slater, Jim
early career with Svend Dohm 160–1
Slim, Lord
defines integrity 82
Sloan, A. P. 123, 162
Smiles, Samuel
Self-Help 141
Smuts, FM Jan 49–50
Holism and Evolution 49
Speer, Albert 112
Stevenson, Robert Louis 24
Stewart, Dr Rosemary
on managers' activities 9
Stress 12–13, 95
contrasted with work pressure 12
effects of 12–13

Taylor Woodrow 16
Tesla, Nikola 70
Thatcher, Margaret 64–5
Thinking ix–x, xi, 1, 26, 36
as mental therapy 163
conflict between concrete and abstract 58–9, 66–7
developing skills in 153
effective thinker defined 158–9
See also Conceptual thinking, Holistic thinking and Imaginative thinking
Thomson, Roy ix, 31, 55, 102, 123, 125, 162
After I was Sixty 103
method of control 56
on need to think 104, 105

on value of argument 124
on value of experience 103–4, 105
on value of stimulation 163–4
Thucydides 126
Tin-opener 126
Tolstoy, Leo
    War and Peace 74
Toyota Motor Co., Japan
    Quality Circles in 150
Trans World Airlines 154
Tull, Jethro
    invention of seed drill 145

US Marine Corps 119

Valuing 23, 25, 82–3, 159
    autonomy of 83–4, 86
    belief in existence of truth 84–7
    consulting specialists 87–90
    in perspective 90–1

Wain, John
    defence of examinations 31

Walter Reed Army Institute of
    Research
    executive monkey experiment
        11–12
Weinstock, Lord 17, 55
    method of control 55
    reduces costs of TV manufacture
        144
Whymper, Edward
    clear thinking by 136
Wilson, Sir Horace 89
Workmate 143
Wright brothers
    fly first aeroplane 144

Younger, W. F.
    on conflict between management
        and work floor vocabularies
        59–60
    on management failure to inspire
        work force 18

Zen 104–5
Zip fastener 142